KT-454-588

Foreword by Peter D. Sutherland

Can the Celtic Tiger cross the Irish Border?

JOHN BRADLEY

and

ESMOND BIRNIE

Cork University Press

in association with

The Centre for Cross Border Studies, Armagh

First published in 2001 by
Cork University Press
University College
Cork
Ireland

THE LIBRARIAN
LETTERKENNY INSTITUTE OF TECHNOLOGY
PORT ROAD,
LETTERKENNY,
CO. DONEGAL.

© Peter D. Sutherland 2001

© John Bradley 2001

© Esmond Birnie 2001

All rights reserved. No part of this book may be reprinted
or reproduced or utilized in any electronic, mechanical or other
means, now known or hereafter invented, including photocopying and
recording or otherwise, without either the prior written permission
of the Publishers or a licence permitting restricted copying in
Ireland issued by the Irish Copyright Licensing Agency Ltd,
The Irish Writers' Centre, 19 Parnell Square, Dublin 1.

British Library Cataloguing in Publication Data
A CIP catalogue record for this book is available from
the British Library

ISBN 1 85918 312 3

Typeset by Tower Books, Ballincollig, Co. Cork
Printed by Colour Books Ltd., Baldoyle, Dublin

LYIT
4002307
LIBRARY
LETTERKENNY

Contents

Foreword

PETER D. SUTHERLAND

*Chairman and MD of Goldman Sachs International and
Non-Executive Chairman of BP Amoco Plc*

I think it relevant to preface my remarks on North-South economic links with a reference to a broader European experience. Following World War II the concept of European integration was significantly linked to economic factors. In fact its success has transformed relationships on our continent without threatening the extremely sensitive European issues of identity. Nobody today can seriously argue that the creation of a single market throughout the European Union in goods, services, capital and people has altered in one iota the sense we all have of who we are and where we come from.

Europeans remain French, German, Spanish and so on as they did before. Their identities, if threatened at all, are threatened by the ubiquity of the potted culture of Hollywood. The rationale for the Treaty of Paris (creating the Coal and Steel Community in 1951) and then the Treaty of Rome (creating the European Economic Community in 1957) was both political and economic. In each respect far more has been achieved than their founding fathers might have expected. The common interests now shared, and the personal interplay stimulated, have not merely reconfigured the map of Europe, creating in particular a single external political identity in trade matters, they have reconfigured attitudes between Europeans. We may retain stereotypes in our minds, but the harshness of our judgements of our neighbours in many cases has undergone a subtle but real change. Also our young feel in a real sense European as well as nationals of their home place.

It has been profoundly disturbing that until relatively recently we in Ireland failed to take any advantage from this European experience. The situation in which we found ourselves following our accession to the EEC in 1973 should have provided us with a tool both for reconciliation and for economic growth on the island. Far from using the example provided for us by the EEC, we appeared to view accession to this large European market as having relevance only to economic relationships abroad rather than between both parts of the island. The evidence of a lack of vision in political quarters was all too obvious. All one had to do was to look at the state of the Dublin to Belfast road, on the southern side of the border particularly, to see the apparent practical irrelevance to policy-makers in Dublin of the opportunity presented by common membership of the EEC.

There were, of course, those who saw the potential advantages of greater economic integration, not merely to ameliorate tensions in the North over the longer term, but also to generate employment in both North and South. (Sir George Quigley deserves specific reference in this regard.) The fact that the word 'integrate' as used in this context ought not to be seen as challenging, from a political or identity point of view, to the Northern majority, appears to have been fairly generally accepted. This was not therefore the main reason for the very limited progress in taking advantage of both being part of a Common Market. It was essentially a failure to match rhetoric with real actions and perhaps a failure of vision.

Today things are quite different. The forces of economic activity themselves have proved too powerful to be resisted. With consolidation in industry and services happening across the borders between major EU partners, it is ridiculous to expect North and South to remain economically separate. Even the ownership of Irish companies no longer truly matters. The larger ones are owned largely by institutional shareholders who could be located anywhere. So if Allied Irish Banks or Independent Newspapers invest in the North through acquisition, this is ultimately merely an exercise by shareholders of an economic choice – I think most people know this and that maximising the small local scale of a market of the whole of Ireland makes sense. So also must greater co-operation between North and South in a whole range of issues from inducing foreign direct investment to developing positions of joint concern in relation to EU policies. Tourism is another obvious example where co-operation can be useful and practically advantageous.

The Island Economy: Past, Present and Future

JOHN BRADLEY

Introduction

The idea of promoting island-wide economic growth and development has received much coverage in recent years, against the background of the evolving peace process in Northern Ireland. As people on both sides of the border begin to accept that there are likely to be mutual gains to be had from more cross-border interactions and co-operation, there is increased attention directed at identifying and removing any remaining barriers and constraints to promoting island-wide growth.

The Good Friday Agreement, signed on April 10th, 1998, contained a specific Strand relating to North-South institutional co-operative arrangements (Strand Two) which potentially had wide implications for public policy. A joint statement, issued on December 18th, 1998 by First Minister David Trimble and Deputy First Minister Seamus Mallon of the Northern Ireland Assembly, set out six implementation bodies for joint North-South policy making and designated six further areas for North-South co-operation of a less formal kind. These cross-border bodies are up and functioning and a week seldom passes without reports of Northern and Southern ministers meeting on matters of common interest. As a result, minds are now becoming much more focused on the practicalities that will be involved if functional areas for

North-South co-operation are to be used to greatest mutual economic and social benefit.

Looking back at the negotiations that eventually led to the institutional arrangements contained in Strand Two of the Good Friday Agreement, it is interesting to note that the main nationalist parties on the island — both in Northern Ireland and in the Republic of Ireland — advocated the desirability of strong North-South links across a broad range of policy areas, in particular those of a business and socio-economic nature. They also advocated the establishment of institutions and structures to develop these links. There were many other under-currents of influence on the nationalist parties as they pursued these goals, but business and policy pragmatism were not entirely absent.

In contrast, the unionist parties within Northern Ireland appeared to be less convinced of the benefits claimed for greater North-South policy and institutional links, often arguing that the economic benefits were likely to be small, if not non-existent. However, it is difficult to establish the extent to which their behaviour was driven by political *desiderata* as distinct from detailed business and economic analysis. Nevertheless, as we watch the cross-border institutions begin to function, it is gratifying to see pragmatism reasserting itself, political fears begin to fade, and unionist ministers engaging actively with their opposite numbers in the South.

Influenced no doubt by the strong performance of the Southern economy over the past decade, recent unionist thinking on the potential benefits of North-South co-operation in the economic sphere has become more flexible. For example, in an address to the Chamber of Commerce of Ireland in Dublin in 1998, First Minister

David Trimble laid down three principles that his party would apply in evaluating cross-border bodies:

1. Any new body should have demonstrable advantages both for Northern Ireland and the Republic of Ireland;
2. Northern Ireland's ability to develop a vibrant and competitive economy on a sound basis should not be impaired;
3. Northern Ireland's identity should not be submerged in a new all-Ireland identity.

The political tensions between differing institutional approaches to the modalities of cross-border co-operation are all too apparent, and the wisdom and salience of such arrangements are vigorously debated within the wider unionist community. However, the most positive and optimistic viewpoint on the potential of deeper business relations between North and South came in a non-political context from within the Northern business community. This was most dramatically articulated by Sir George Quigley in an address to the Confederation of Irish Industry conference in 1992, when he said that: 'I find no difficulty with the proposition that Ireland is — or should be — an island economy'.

This simple and clear statement gave a considerable boost to many in the business community, especially in Northern Ireland, who had been slowly and pragmatically increasing North-South trade and business links on the island. The statement also had a galvanising impact on how business people, policy-makers and academics began to think about the opportunities that a peaceful future might bring to the economies of Ireland, North and South, especially in the context of increasing European integration. The fact that Sir George Quigley's statement was regarded as very *avant garde* in 1992 indicates just how far thinking has advanced since then. At about the same time, the Joint Business Council of the Confederation of Irish Industry (now the Irish Business and Employers Confederation — IBEC) in the South and the Confederation of British Industry in the North was formed, and has played an important part in encouraging and facilitating significant increases in the level of trade, business contacts, development and co-operation between both parts of Ireland.

It might be thought that there is already an island economy within the context of the Single European Market. After all, both the United Kingdom and the Republic of Ireland are member states of the EU. If there are still problems, what is it about the island of Ireland that makes it different from the mainstream processes of EU market integration, requiring more specific analysis and initiatives in addition to those common to normal cross-border relations in other EU member states?

Policy-making in Ireland prior to 1922 took place in a context where the island as a whole was an integral part of the United Kingdom. The impact of the Government of Ireland Act of 1920 on subsequent policy-making in the two regional economies of the island was to create two separate policy regimes. However, traces of the earlier policy legacy, in the form of adherence to many UK policy norms, also lasted in the South until well into the 1960s. Stormont, on the other hand, never really exploited, developed, or even tested the limits of its regional policy autonomy.

The impact of direct rule after the prorogation of Stormont in 1972 worked towards an even closer integration of Northern Ireland into the UK at the very time when the Republic of Ireland was switching its political and economic focus away from London and towards Brussels. However, Irish and UK membership of the EU after 1973 provided a context for the removal of all tariff barriers between North and South, a process that had got under way as long ago as 1965 with the signing of the Anglo-Irish Free Trade Agreement.[1] The Single European Market of 1992 was designed to remove all non-tariff barriers between EU member states and hence between the Republic of Ireland and Northern Ireland. Economic and Monetary Union (EMU) has the potential for further policy harmonisation between the Republic of Ireland and the UK, should the UK eventually join.[2] Thus, political and economic currents have resulted in the North-South policy-making environment today having a high — if less than complete — degree of commonality.

The scope for loss of economic efficiency due to lack of full market completion between Northern Ireland and the Republic of Ireland has diminished considerably with the advent and later deepening of the EU Single Market. However, the completion of the island market still remains unfinished and any adverse effects of lack of completion — such as the UK not joining the euro zone — are compounded by political sensitivities that persist within Northern Ireland, between North and South, and between the UK and the Republic of Ireland. This legacy has served to sustain opposing views on the possible gains to be had from continued market completion and the possible evolution of an island economy, ranging from a conviction that the commercial benefits of further policy co-operation or harmonisation would be minimal (expressed in the writings of the Cadogan Group — a unionist think-tank — as well as those of Paddy Roche, Esmond Birnie and David Hitchens) to the suggestion that there may be many remaining problem areas and barriers specific to the economy of this island, the removal of which would be likely to create more dynamic growth and prosperity (expressed most succinctly by Sir George Quigley).

Although the evolution of the framework of the EU treaties has also diminished the scope for policy mismatch between member states, considerable policy misalignment still remains in areas such as fiscal and monetary policy, taxation, industrial policy, social welfare, education, labour market, infrastructure and agriculture. The extent to which any loss in efficiency and under-performance can be associated with mismatch in public policy needs to be investigated, particularly when the two regions involved share an extended land border and have a relatively high level of inter-regional trade and factor mobility. Although one can draw on wider inter-country EU experience and research findings, a specific focus needs to be directed at the Irish-UK policy interface in the context of the two economies of the island of Ireland, since policy regimes in Northern Ireland are almost completely dominated by UK policy norms.

We also need to understand the manner in which institutional harmonisation might moderate the effects of barriers and encourage mutually beneficial opportunities for North-South growth and development. Current interest has, understandably, focused on the likely impact of institutional harmonisation in the main sectors of the island economy (i.e. agriculture, energy, trade, transport and communications) where policy-making often involves large publicly-owned, semi-state and privatised organisations as well as government departments and, increasingly, independent regulation. These make up the institutional context described in Strand Two of the Good Friday Agreement and form part of the agreement of December 18th, 1998 on Northern government departments, North-South implementation bodies and co-operation.

Harmonisation and co-operation in wider areas of economic life, such as industrial policy, joint planning of physical infrastructure, consumer affairs and approaches to EU policy-making, may be important in promoting island-wide growth, but operate mainly through medium to long-term (and often indirect) channels. Social policy aspects of cross-border co-operation are not our main concern, but it is important to understand the full extent to which existing North-South socio-economic differences may have created barriers to mutually beneficial growth, and how harmonisation and co-operation in these areas might act to mitigate or remove them. Political and cultural issues also divide Northern Ireland in a way that has implications for the performance of the Northern economy and for North-South business and economic interactions, but it is for others to examine these aspects and prescribe remedies.

Our analysis is designed to investigate the barriers to accelerated growth and development in the island economy of Ireland that arise from what we characterise as partial market completion and the policy mismatch associated with the existence of an international border between the Republic of Ireland and Northern Ireland. As noted above, some of these problems are common to all regions of nation states that have international land borders and are the subject of discussion and analysis at the EU level. However, the Irish situation has some unusual and unique features:

1. A history of mistrust and lack of communication between the two regions that has only recently begun to unfreeze and change;
2. The geographically peripheral location of both regions with respect to their core markets in Britain, the rest of the EU and elsewhere;
3. Asymmetries in the roles and power of policy-making institutions in both regions that have made previous North-South co-operation difficult to foster;
4. Regional economic structures that have evolved in different ways within the island, reflecting among other things their different external relationships — Northern Ireland with London and the Republic of Ireland increasingly with Brussels and Frankfurt.

This essay is structured as follows. Since historical context is all-important in developing an understanding of Irish issues, we briefly review the background history to the two island economies since we are still — at least to some degree — constrained by our history. We then turn to the state of the two economies today and show that one fortuitous consequence of the last decade of fast growth in the Republic of Ireland is that the two economies face each other across the border with a much greater degree of social and economic parity than they have done at any time since partition. We then direct our attention to the future and engage in some informed speculation about what the island economy might look like in ten or twenty years from now, at a time when we may look back at the Good Friday Agreement as a turning point in the fortunes of our island and a harbinger of peace, stability and prosperity. Finally, we draw some general conclusions.

The Island Economy of the Past

In his illuminating account of the post-war success of Japan, the economist Mikio Morishima felt it necessary to go back to the fourth century! We do not need to go back quite so far in order to understand how the island economy came to be in its present state, but we do need to revisit some of the consequences of the Act of Union, 1800. One such consequence in the late 19th century was the emergence of a North-South divide on the island, into a prosperous industrial North-East and a poor agricultural South. Even after partition in 1920, this divide continued to influence the external orientation and economic possibilities on both sides of the border, and the legacy of the earlier period has only recently been overcome at the end of the 20th century.

Ireland's industrialisation never emulated Britain's generalised economic and technological leap forward. Rather, it involved a few specific sectors (brewing, linen, shipbuilding), and selected locations (mainly Belfast and Dublin), and by-passed much of the rest of the country. What is of interest is that the concentration of the key sectors, linen and shipbuilding, came to be located almost exclusively in the north-east corner of the island. The greater Belfast region took on all the attributes of an 'industrial district', i.e. a geographically defined economy characterised by a large number of firms that are involved at various stages and in various ways in the production of closely inter-related products.[3] Population grew in the area around

Belfast, to the extent that by 1911, the population of the Belfast area had outstripped that of Dublin.

The South embarked on a path of political independence after 1922 with an economy that was without significant industrialisation and dependent on mainly agricultural exports to the British market. The North achieved a degree of regional autonomy within the UK at a stage when the perilous state of its strong industrial base was still hidden in the aftermath of the economic boom created by the First World War.

Between 1921 and the early 1960s there were many changes North and South, but few of major significance compared with the legacy of the pre-1922 period. The South attempted to construct an industrial base behind a protective barrier of high tariffs. The North's staple industrial specialisations continued to decline, with a temporary period of growth during and immediately after the Second World War. Both regions entered the 1960s in a state where major policy changes were needed, even though the North had been moderately successful during the 1950s in attracting British investment in the areas of textiles, artificial fibres and other petroleum-based products. What was not anticipated was that the outbreak of civil unrest would make this transformation much more prolonged and difficult than it would have been in a period of peaceful economic transition.

The mid 20th century features of the island economy had clear origins in the early and middle of the 19th century. These included a weak island industrial base, other than in the north-east corner of the island; the interaction of population growth with weak economic performance that was to appear as a mixture of unemployment/under-employment and emigration; a vicious circle of interaction between emigration and a weak ability to create a national system of innovation; and an almost complete integration into and dependence on the British economy. Only after a period of national crisis was a sustained effort made in the South to address these problems, beginning with the publication of *The First Programme for Economic Expansion* in 1958. It was to be a long haul, and the fruits of success were not to become available until the 1990s. Parallel efforts made in the North during the 1950s and 1960s produced a rate of Northern industrial-based growth that for a short while exceeded that of Britain. However, subsequent efforts were hampered by a lack of appropriate regional policy instruments and by the effects of the outbreak and persistence of civil unrest that lasted from the late 1960s until the cease-fires of the early 1990s.

The Island Economy Today

Radical transformations have taken place during the past three decades in both economies of the island, introducing dramatic differences in the relative performance of North and South. Overlaying these differences is the civil unrest (or so-called 'troubles') that casts a shadow over the recent economic development of Northern Ireland. A detailed discussion of the reasons for the stronger performance of the South relative to the North in the last decade would require a separate book.[4] Basically five key factors are involved in the South's dynamic performance: the steady build-up of human capital after the educational reforms in the 1960s; the major improvements in physical infrastructure, particularly since 1989, as a result of the EU Structural

Funds; the extreme openness of the economy and its export orientation to fast-growing markets and products, together with benefits stemming from the completion of the Single European Market and from massive foreign direct investment inflows; the changing demographic structure and the role of inward migration in preventing skill shortages; and the stable domestic macroeconomic policy environment.

The role played by large-scale British financial support in sustaining the standard of living in the North has perhaps served to mask the true nature of the differences in performance between North and South. The situation in the North would appear to be rather less advantageous than in the South for each of the above five factors. The problems associated with the selectivity of the Northern education system and the effective exclusion of many from higher education are beginning to be understood. Economic openness is less beneficial to the North than is the case in the South, since the North's export orientation is mainly to the slower growing British markets and to more traditional products. The overhang of the large financial subvention and fears about its possible reduction have introduced uncertainty to Northern medium-term economic planning. Northern demographic trends remain out of line with the European norms to which the South has converged. In fact the only exception where the relative position of the North is better than the South is in the state of physical infrastructure, and this is changing rapidly.

We turn our attention now to some of the main features of the economies of both regions as they are today. We first examine the issues of relative standards of living, and then comment on the wider performance of both economies.

Relative standards of living

Comparisons of the present state of the economies of North and South can be made for a variety of reasons. A simple reason might spring from a desire to rank both regions in a performance league table with a view to deciding which was the more 'successful' in some sense yet to be defined. A more pragmatic reason might be to seek to understand better the current and likely future performance of either or both regions with a view to exploiting trade and other business opportunities between them.

We can illustrate some aspects of these issues by first looking at the levels of national output (more precisely, GDP at factor cost) per head in the North and South (Table 1).[5]

Table 1: GDP at factor cost per head: Northern Ireland and the Republic of Ireland

	1990	1991	1992	1993	1994	1995	1996
NI (£)	6,396	6,930	7,205	7,620	7,974	8,423	8,700
RoI (£IR)	6,907	7,192	7,545	8,177	8,720	9,703	10,591
RoI (£)	6,425	6,567	7,313	7,984	8,526	9,863	10,863
NI/RoI	1.00	1.06	0.99	0.95	0.94	0.85	0.80

Source: Data for Northern Ireland are taken from Table 12.1 of *Regional Trends 33*, 1998 edition, ONS. Data for the Republic of Ireland are taken from Table 3 of *National Income and Expenditure 1997*. Conversion of £IR to sterling uses annual average exchange rates taken from the *Quarterly Reports of the Central Bank of Ireland*. No alteration is made for differences in relative cost-of-living (i.e, purchasing power parity).

Starting off in the year 1990 at about parity in terms of national output per head, and ignoring the anomaly in the year 1991, the trend has been for the Republic of Ireland to move systematically ahead of Northern Ireland in terms of this measure of performance. By the year 1996, the gap between North and South had risen to 20 per cent.

However, although GDP at factor cost is a useful measure of the value of goods produced in each region, and is closely related to employment and investment activity in production, it is not a very good measure of income accruing to the inhabitants of either region, since there are leakages of funds out of, as well as inflows into, each region from abroad.[6] The main outflows from the Republic of Ireland consist of that element of profits made by foreign multinational firms which is repatriated, as well as interest payments made to foreign holders of Irish national debt. Inflows arise mainly from payments from abroad made to private citizens as well as from funding associated with the EU (mainly CAP subsidies and Structural Funds). These inflows and outflows are measured in the Irish National Accounts and permit the construction of an aggregate measure of economic activity that more accurately reflects how much income remains within the domestic economy, i.e. GNP or gross *national* product.[7]

Since research by the Northern Ireland Economic Council has shown that a considerable portion of Northern manufacturing and services is also externally owned, it is clear that there must be significant outflows of profits from Northern Ireland to Britain, the USA and elsewhere. Unfortunately these are not measured officially. On the other hand, some of the main inflows are recorded and published, and consist of the so-called 'subvention' from Britain (by far the largest element) as well as funding from the EU (mainly agricultural (CAP) subsidies, Structural Funds and the Peace and Reconciliation funds), which is a relatively minor consideration.

A better measure of relative welfare North and South that is published in both regions is provided by the level of Personal Disposable Income (PDI) per head of population. PDI measures income of the personal sector (i.e. households, other individuals and non-profit-making bodies serving persons), after deduction of all direct taxes on income. Table 2 shows this for the years 1990-96, since official data are not presently available after 1996.

Table 2: Personal disposable income per head: Northern Ireland and the Republic of Ireland

	1990	1991	1992	1993	1994	1995	1996
NI (£)	5,767	6,385	6,839	7,208	7,537	7,960	8,181
RoI (£IR)	5,196	5,498	5,798	6,119	6,389	6,799	7,165
RoI (£)	4,833	5,021	5,619	5,975	6,247	6,911	7,349
NI/RoI	1.19	1.27	1.22	1.21	1.21	1.15	1.11

Source: Data for Northern Ireland are taken from Table 12.7 of *Regional Trends 33*, 1998 edition, ONS. Data for the Republic of Ireland are taken from Table 9 of *National Income and Expenditure 1997*. Conversion of £IR to sterling uses annual average exchange rates taken from the *Quarterly Reports of the Central Bank of Ireland*. No adjustment is made for differences in relative cost-of-living (i.e. purchasing power parity).

Since personal disposable income can be used either for consumption or savings, one would expect that the levels of consumption per head North and South would mirror the levels of income per head, and Table 3 shows that this is broadly the case.

Table 3: Household consumption per head: Northern Ireland and the Republic of Ireland

	1994	1995	1996
NI (£)	6,357	6,916	7,409
RoI (£IR)	5,732	6,065	6,477
RoI (£)	5,605	6,165	6,643
NI/RoI	1.13	1.12	1.12

Source: Data for Northern Ireland are taken from Table 12.8 of *Regional Trends 33*, 1998 edition, ONS. Data for the Republic of Ireland are taken from Table 5 of *National Income and Expenditure 1997*. Conversion of £IR to sterling uses annual average exchange rates taken from the *Quarterly Reports of the Central Bank of Ireland*. No adjustment is made for differences in relative cost-of-living (i.e. purchasing power parity).

On the basis of personal disposable income per head, in 1996 the average person in Northern Ireland was about £832 (or 11 per cent) better off than the average person in the Republic of Ireland. The North-South differential in personal disposable income has declined from a value of £934 per head in 1990 or a percentage difference of around 20 per cent. Since the consumer price level rose in the North by 11.2 per cent more than in the South between 1990 and 1996 (see Table 4 below), in simple real purchasing terms the PDI differential in 1996 was about £750 per head or just over 10 per cent in the North's favour.[8] With growth in the South far outstripping that in the North since 1996, it is likely that a further narrowing of the PDI differential has occurred and that, at least according to this indicator of average living standards, the South will probably overtake the North in the very near future unless Northern private sector growth accelerates or unless the per capita subvention rate is increased.

Table 4: Comparative average growth rates for Northern Ireland and the Republic of Ireland 1990–96

	Northern Ireland	Republic of Ireland
GDP (nominal)	42.3% (6.1% pa)	57.7% (7.9% pa)
GDP (real)	16.1% (2.5% pa)	31.9% (4.7% pa)
Consumer prices	25.7% (3.9% pa)	14.5% (2.3% pa)
Total employment	4.3% (1.007% pa)	16.0% (2.5% pa)

Sources: Regional Trends, various issues; Economic Trends Annual Supplement, 1997, for Northern Ireland. UK-wide deflators are used for Northern Ireland with no adjustment for sectoral composition. NIE, 1997 and LFS, 1997 for the Republic of Ireland.

One might be tempted to attribute the differential in favour of Northern Ireland to the superior economic performance of the Northern economy, and in a certain highly qualified sense this is true. However, if we define regional performance net of external transfers, then a rather different picture emerges. The 'subvention' paid by the UK government to Northern Ireland in recent years (i.e. the difference between revenue raised in or attributed to Northern Ireland and public expenditure) amounted in 1995 to just over £2,000 per person.[9] The fact that Northern Ireland is politically a region of the UK means that it attracts this subvention automatically from being part of the UK fiscal union. However, such a high level of subvention is needed for Northern Ireland only because – as demonstrated by UK regional research — without the subvention its economic performance has been and remains poor compared to the other ten standard UK regions.

The Republic of Ireland, on the other hand, attracts no such subvention, but does receive generous investment aid from the EU under the Structural Funds (or Community Support Framework), as well as agricultural subsidy payments through the CAP.[10] However, depending on whether or not one includes the CAP subsidy payments with the CSF for the case of the Republic of Ireland, these are between 5 times (including them) and 9 times (excluding them) smaller per person per year than the NI subvention.[11] With the winding down of Structural Funds between 2000-2006, the ratio is now even bigger.

Hence, in any comparison of the economies of Northern Ireland and the Republic of Ireland, policy differences that arise due to differences in governance must be kept in mind. Simplistic and unqualified comparisons of economic indicators tend to be misleading and generate fruitless debate. More detailed comparisons can be more informative if the objective is to explore the ability of the regional private sector to compete in external markets and to lessen the dependence on external public finance. However, one should not be too dogmatic about the conclusions since the welfare as well as the political issues are complex. Nevertheless, the implications of severe regional imbalances in public finances and their consequences for the relative sizes of the public and private sectors in a region eventually lead to problems of dependency. In nation states they either lead to policy feed-backs that restore balance to the public finances or, in the absence of appropriate policy responses, they can ultimately lead to loss of economic sovereignty.

North-South strengths and weaknesses

As a prelude to consideration of how matters might improve, it is useful to summarise the strengths and weaknesses of both economies as they are today. In the case of Northern Ireland, a series of structural weaknesses in the economy is to some extent a legacy of the past industrial strength of the region. They have three main characteristics. First, there is a continued dependence on the traditional sectors like textiles, shipbuilding, clothing and footwear, which are particularly vulnerable to low-cost competition and changing demand. Second, there is a deficit in education levels (particularly at the middle and lower ends) that contributes to low productivity and high structural unemployment. Third, a structural dependence on the public sector to sustain employment has emerged as a consequence of an inability to attract high quality foreign direct investment in sufficient quantity to offset the decline in domestic traditional industry.

The difficulties experienced by policy-makers in attempting to address these problems are reasonably well understood. There has been an unwillingness (or inability) of the Northern Ireland authorities to make a break with previous areas of specialisation. There is only very limited degree of policy autonomy within NI, and this effectively prevented the emergence of region-specific policy variations from national policies designed to address region-specific structural problems. Finally, the disruption caused by violent conflict – together with related problems of increased labour market segmentation and discrimination – made it much more difficult to mobilise resources of both private capital and labour to bring about fundamental changes.

LYIT LIBRARY
400 23107
LETTERKENNY

A very different pattern of behaviour has been experienced in the Republic of Ireland. Here, the main background factors underlying present growth could be summarised as follows. Exercising its policy autonomy, there was a dramatic break with protectionist policies from the late 1950s, and much of the artificially sustained inefficient indigenous industry was subsequently allowed to fail. A tax-based competitive environment was created that was attractive to foreign direct investment, while simultaneously working to improve the level of domestic physical infrastructure and human capital. This policy, after a slow start in the 1960s, eventually proved to be spectacularly successful by the mid-1990s, to the extent that about 60 per cent of manufacturing output in the Republic of Ireland is now produced by foreign-owned multinational enterprises. Finally, the economy of the Republic of Ireland was largely untouched by the destructive and disruptive aspects of the Northern violence. Where costs associated with conflict-related spillovers had to be borne, they were containable and mainly in the areas of increased security in border areas.

A period of peace is necessary to facilitate structural reform and change, and should permit the Northern Ireland economy to accelerate its growth and development. However, the existence of two economies on the island of Ireland is likely to impose constraints on this process unless barriers are identified and removed. We now turn to consideration of barriers that arise due to market failure and policy mismatch.

The Island Economy of the Future

Strategic issues

In a wide strategic context, the two regions of the island appear to be characterised by very different economic policy environments as they plan for their futures. In the case of the Republic of Ireland, its strategic policy orientation towards the future is relatively benign at present and could be characterised in terms of five key issues. First is the continued creative use of its modest but significant scope for national policy-making autonomy against a background of a progressive ceding of elements of macroeconomic fiscal and monetary policy autonomy to the institutions of the EU. The second issue is a continuation of the crucial policy orientation of the past decades concerning openness to inward investment using a mainly tax-based system of industrial incentives and associated improvements in physical infrastructure and human capital. Thirdly, further modernisation of the industrial base through targeted foreign direct investment in high technology areas as well as through steady expansion of indigenously-owned industry is necessary. Fourth is a likely continuation of the process of 'decoupling' of the economy away from the earlier heavy dependence on the UK as a result of its sustained systematic and pro-active orientation towards participation in EU policy initiatives. The fifth issue is the pursuit of steady improvement in economic performance with the aim of converging systematically towards the standard of living of the wealthier core economies of the EU, as well as bringing about greater social equity.

The strategic policy context for Northern Ireland is more difficult to characterise with any degree of precision, since the region has only recently experienced a sustained period of peace and is in the process of designing and implementing major changes to its system of political and economic governance. Nevertheless, from a strategic point of view the region faces major policy challenges and will have to address some potentially serious issues. Most important of these is the continuation into the medium term of a situation where the region has limited regional policy-making autonomy combined with a lack of political consensus as to the wisdom of seeking out and using greater policy autonomy in the context of the Good Friday Agreement. Second is the continued use of a range of policy instruments (particularly in the area of indiscriminate grant-based industrial incentives) that have not proved particularly effective in the past. Thirdly, there are difficulties in modernising its manufacturing base away from its traditional specialities, e.g. textiles and clothing, towards higher value-added products. Fourth is a continuing dependence on Britain as the main external sales destination, with potentially undesirable consequences in terms of slow and erratic growth in the longer term and with the UK remaining outside EMU for the present at least. The fifth issue is economic peripherality within the UK, and one of the lowest standards of living among the UK regions, combined with the possible perpetuation of dependence on external financial aid in the form of the 'subvention', with consequential lack of dynamism in the regional economy (i.e. a *Mezzogiorno* problem).[12]

The fact that the Northern and Southern strategic policy orientations are so out of alignment is likely to have disruptive consequences for planning and executing moves towards the completion of the island market economy. While there are likely to be many positive aspects to the evolution of North-South relationships over the coming years, there will be negative aspects as well. In very general terms, the strategic policy environment of the Republic of Ireland would appear to be more favourable at present than the situation facing Northern Ireland. There remains the possibility that, in the absence of explicit and concerted North-South co-operative initiatives, there will be a tendency for a continuation of the previous process of essentially separate development of the two regions and an inability to complete the island economy, even as conventional North-South trade continues to expand. In the absence of appropriate island-wide policy-making forums, there is likely to be a lack of focus and urgency in addressing the related problems and consequences of policy mismatch. There may be a tendency to accept the continuation of the economic isolation and internal peripherality of the immediate cross-border regions, in particular the north-west region centred on Donegal and Derry, the central region of Armagh, Fermanagh, Sligo, Monaghan, Leitrim and Cavan, and the east border region of Down and Louth, centred on Newry and Dundalk.

In the light of the differing strategic policy-making contexts of North and South, we need to understand how the process of market completion is progressing on the island. Guided by the mainstream EU material from the Cecchini (1988) and the Monti (1997) programmes of Single European Market (SEM) research, it is possible to isolate three main areas of the island economy where market completion continues to be hindered due to the presence of the border.

The first (and most direct) involves the direct spatial disruptive impacts of the physical presence of the border itself. The second concerns the emergence of different industrial structures in Northern Ireland and the Republic of Ireland. The third follows directly from structural mismatch in the industrial area and involves the consequential distorting impact of the border on conventional North-South trade.

Physical border problems

An obvious barrier to the full market completion of the island economy is, of course, the physical existence of the border itself since 1922. The Single Market in the EU has now removed all remaining non-tariff barriers that were border-related, and goods and services can now pass through with little or no disruption other than problems related to security whenever violence resurfaces within Northern Ireland. However, this does not mean that the border has ceased to be of any significance for economic development on the island.

A continuing legacy of the border is that the development of physical infrastructure on the island is a long-drawn-out process, and the disruptive impact of the border is therefore likely to endure for a long time. The physical infrastructure of the island for most of this century was developed within each region in isolation from the other, with little or no account taken until recently of how it could be best co-ordinated to maximise all-island business and economic developmental needs. Moreover, the border has created areas of internal peripherality and cut regions off from their natural economic hinterlands, e.g. the north-west region (centred on Derry) and the north-east region (straddling the border between Newry and Dundalk).

A recent manifestation of the peripherality of Donegal arose in connection with the troubled *Fruit of the Loom* plants there. An (unpublished) report prepared for the IDA stated:

> Despite our efforts, few companies have chosen to locate in the North West region. Our experience of dealing with clients who have located elsewhere has shown us that poor access by air and road, Northern troubles, limited sub-supplier capacity and small urban structure have made the region unattractive in comparison with other locations (*Irish Times*, August 17, 1998).

The consequences of these distorting processes – legacies from a time when cross-border co-operation and policy co-ordination were largely absent – will take some time to rectify. This is where cross-border policies dealing with transport, the environment, waterways, tourism, EU programmes and urban and rural development are likely to initiate major improvements in the nature and quality of social and commercial relationships in the immediate border areas as well as further afield.

Industrial structure

Overall manufacturing employment shares in Northern Ireland and the Republic of Ireland are fairly similar, though the South has a far higher concentration in high technology industries. The Southern situation reflects the much more significant contribution of foreign direct investment, which has raised productivity and profitability substantially. Indirect information on the indigenously owned sectors suggests greater similarity, North and South.

Table 5 shows the manufacturing employment shares for the main UK regions as well as for the Republic of Ireland, disaggregated into three broad sub-sectors: food, drink and tobacco; a traditional sector consisting mainly of textiles, leather and wood products; and the remainder, which consists broadly of modern industries. The similarities between Scotland and the Republic of Ireland are apparent, where both have a higher than average concentration of employment in food, drink and tobacco and a share of modern manufacturing employment that lies between that of England and Wales (at the high end) and Northern Ireland (at the low end).

Table 5: Traditional and modern industry – 1996
employment percentage shares

	UK	England	Wales	Scotland	NI	RoI
Food, drink and tobacco	11.7	11.0	10.5	17.9	18.6	20.5
Traditional	16.4	16.0	14.4	17.6	29.8	15.0
Modern	71.9	73.0	75.1	64.5	51.6	64.5
Total	100	100	100	100	100	100

Source: *Business Monitor*, 1996 for the UK and regions; CIP, 1996 for the Republic of Ireland.

Trade patterns

A key relationship between the economies of Northern Ireland and the Republic of Ireland involves North-South trade. To sell outside a regional economy requires the ability to produce a range of goods and services that are in demand elsewhere. Our characterisation of the

Northern and Southern productive structures — with the South having a more modern industrial base — has important implications for trade. Table 6 shows the export proportions of Southern trade with the North, Britain and the rest of the EU for the year 1997. Table 7 shows similar data for imports.

Table 6: Republic of Ireland: Export shares by destination, 1997

Exports to NI	Exports to Britain	Exports to rest of EU
2.9%	21.4%	45.0%

Source: Trade Statistics, December 1997, CSO.

Table 7: Republic of Ireland: Import shares by origin: 1997

Imports from NI	Imports from Britain	Imports from rest of EU
2.8%	30.9%	24.2%

Source: Trade Statistics, December 1997, CSO.

Data for external sales shares for the North are shown in Table 8. Unfortunately, data on imports by the North are not available since regional data are not collected in the UK.

Table 8: Northern Ireland: External sales by
destination, 1996/97

Sales to Britain	Exports to RoI	Exports to rest of EU
50.7%	9.6%	20.6%

Source: *Made in Northern Ireland Sold to the World*, NIERC/DED/IDB, 1998

These tables show that exports from the South to the North account for about 3 per cent of total Southern exports, while exports from the North to the South account for almost 10 per cent of total external sales.[13] In other words, the South is over three times more important as an export market for Northern firms than the North is as an export market for Southern firms. On the other hand, Britain is over twice as important a market for Northern firms as it is for Southern firms, which are more oriented towards trade with the rest of the EU. Britain is more important for the South as a source of imports than it is as a destination for exports, i.e. the South runs a trade deficit with Britain. However, the South runs a trade surplus with the North, which totalled about £IR300 million for the year 1997.

To explore the details of bilateral North-South trade we can use the detailed trade statistics produced by the Irish Central Statistics Office. Table 9 shows Southern exports to the North, to Britain and to the entire EU, disaggregated using the Standard Industrial Trade Classification (SITC), with specific details of some sub-divisions. The table highlights some striking facts. Exports from the South to the North are heavily concentrated in SITC 0 (Food and Live Animals), accounting for 24.5 per cent of total Southern exports to Northern Ireland. For the same product category, this compares with 17 per cent of total exports to Britain and only 11 per cent of total exports to the EU as a whole.

There is a very high concentration of Southern exports in categories SITC 7 (Machinery and Transport Equipment) to Britain and the EU as a whole, accounting for over a third in each, but only 12 per cent of total Southern SITC 7 exports to the North. More notably, for the important category of SITC 75 (Office and ADP machines), almost 25 per cent of Southern exports to Britain and to the EU fall into this category but less than 2 per cent of total exports to the North.

The situation for SITC 5 (Chemicals and related products) is also anomalous, but not quite as dramatic as the previous cases, with 24 per cent of total exports to EU in this category, 16 per cent to Britain, but only 9 per cent to the North. One should note a residual category – 'Other' – which makes up 15 per cent of total Southern exports to the North, and is negligible to anywhere else. This category consists of goods whose trade volume is at too low a threshold to be accurately recorded, and almost certainly consists of traditional rather than high technology products. Table 10 gives the corresponding data for shares of Southern imports from the North, from Britain and from the EU as a whole. It is clear that Southern imports from the North are very heavily concentrated in SITC 0 (Food and Live Animals), accounting for 25 per cent of total imports, compared to 9 per cent from Britain and the EU.

The importance of Southern imports from Britain and from the EU in SITC 7 (Machinery and Transport Equipment) is clear, with one-third of the total from each, but only 8 per cent from the North. In SITC 75 (Office and ADP machines) and 77 (Instruments), Southern imports from the North have a very low share of the total of imports from the North. This pattern is repeated, though less dramatically, for SITC 5 (Chemicals).

If one defines 'traditional' products as SITC sections 0, 6, 8 and 'Other', then about 73 per cent of total Southern imports from the North fall into this category. The corresponding figures for Southern imports from Britain and from the EU are only 46.1 and 41 per cent, respectively.

Table 9: Republic of Ireland export shares by SITC sections: 1997

SITC	Exports to NI* (percentage of total)	Exports to Britain* (percentage of total)	Exports to EU* (percentage of total)
0	24.5	16.9	11.3
1	6.6	1.7	1.6
2	2.8	2.2	1.8
3	1.1	1.0	0.6
4	0.0	0.2	0.1
5	9.3	15.9	24.4
(54)	*(0.8)*	*4.2*	*(5.6)*
6	17.4	5.6	4.4
7	12.1	36.8	35.6
(75)	*(1.8)*	*(25.1)*	*(23.8)*
(77)	*(1.9)*	*(5.9)*	*(6.4)*
8	12.0	14.8	15.0
9	0.0	3.1	3.9
Other	15.3	1.8	1.3

Source: Trade Statistics, December 1997, CSO.
Note: Totals of shares may not add to 100 due to rounding

Table 10: Republic of Ireland import shares by SITC sections: 1997

SITC	Exports to NI* (percentage of total)	Exports to Britain* (percentage of total)	Exports to EU* (percentage of total)
0	24.7	9.2	9.1
1	7.2	0.9	1.7
2	2.4	0.9	1.5
3	1.2	5.8	3.4
4	0.0	0.6	0.5
5	8.2	13.6	15.4
(54)	*(0.6)*	*(2.7)*	*(2.6)*
6	25.5	17.0	15.7
7	8.5	31.8	34.7
(75)	*(2.2)*	*(7.5)*	*(8.4)*
(77)	*(1.2)*	*(9.0)*	*(7.7)*
8	10.5	15.3	13.0
9	0.0	1.2	2.0
Other	11.8	3.7	3.0

Source: Trade Statistics, December 1997, CSO.
Note: Totals of shares may not add to 100 due to rounding

Thus, the composition of bilateral trade between the North and the South is very different from bilateral trade between Britain and the South, as well as between the EU as a whole and the South. North-South trade – both ways – is predominantly in traditional, low technology products with an exceptionally high weight for SITC 0 (Food, Drink and Tobacco). This phenomenon has not received the attention it deserves, but of course simply reflects the underlying industrial structure in Northern Ireland compared with the Republic of

Ireland. We saw earlier in this section that the two industrial structures are very different, the South having a concentration in modern high technology sectors, and the North specialising in more traditional sectors. However, the most important dynamic promoting increased intra-EU trade in the Single Market of the EU is associated inter-firm trade in similar product areas rather than trade in finished consumer goods. This two-way trade simply cannot easily take place between North and South, given the contrasting production structures.

The future of North-South trade

With an improved political situation in the North, recent experience shows that the previous reluctance of individuals and groups to travel freely between both regions is declining. Greatly increased North-South tourist flows, and the pressure on the limited capacity of the Belfast-Dublin road and rail links, bear testimony to this process of North-South development. However, there remain other important reasons for continued market segmentation such as the very different industrial structures, different fiscal and monetary/exchange rate regimes, and the separate and parallel functioning of public sector development agencies like the IDA and Enterprise Ireland in the South and the IDB and LEDU in the North, with their obvious implications for higher business transactions costs when working in both markets.

It is heartening to note that rapid progress is being made in addressing the problem of North-South market segmentation. Trade literature in the South is now disseminating information on Northern marketing opportunities. An ambitious joint initiative of An Bord Tráchtála (now Enterprise Ireland) and the Northern Ireland Industrial

Development Board, supported by the International Fund for Ireland, has resulted in the publication of a detailed marketing guide to fifteen key product areas, facilitating greater North-South trade penetration as well as providing opportunities for import substitution. Joint promotions of Irish products overseas have been organised, and strategic alliances are being encouraged between Northern and Southern firms. The distribution system on the island, which has tended to deal with the North as part of the UK and with the South as a separate region, is gradually being integrated on an island basis. In the longer term, the development of strategic transport links on an integrated all-island basis would be a powerful force for removing North-South market segmentation. Finally, the recently agreed North-South Implementation Bodies include a major initiative on Trade and Business Development.

The potential gains from greater North-South trade interaction, given existing Northern industrial activity, may be modest relative to the potential gains from greater penetration into wider world markets, including British markets. Nevertheless, there are gains to be made from intra-island trade in circumstances that will assist in strengthening the competitive performance of all businesses on this island. North-South trade improvement on this island is not an *alternative* to East-West trade improvement, but is entirely *complementary* to it. It is a transitional process that will produce gains in the short term and, by strengthening its supply side, will help to position the island economy to make further advances in world markets. North-South trade will reach its potential if and only if the structure of manufacturing in Northern Ireland can be modernised and brought into line with that of Wales and Scotland.

The euro and North-South economics

As in the case of fiscal policy, the North has no scope for an independent monetary policy. Hence, the impact of monetary policy mismatch on cross-border interactions must also be viewed in the light of the UK-Republic of Ireland policy interface. At present, this comes down to the decision of the South to participate in EMU and the decision of the UK to stay out, at least from the start-up phase.

The potential benefits of any currency union consist of reduced transaction costs, lower interest rates, increased price transparency and (if the European Central Bank does its job properly!) lower inflation. Potential costs consist of transitional expenses (cash registers, ATMs, accounting arrangements and price displays); the possibility that so-called 'core' regions will gain at the expense of 'peripheral' regions; the fact that more of the costs of adjustment to adverse shocks will have to be borne by the labour market in the absence of a national exchange rate; the prospect that some sectors may be hit more than others; and (importantly for the peace process), the evolution of North-South business interactions on this island may be hindered by the non-membership of the UK.

Why is there a regional dimension to EMU within the UK? After all, the Maastricht criteria only have meaning at the national level and regions of the UK already share a common currency. But if decisions on EMU are taken with 'national' criteria in mind, the consequences for the regions are unlikely to be uniform. Regional economies within nation states can be and are very heterogeneous. Regions tend to specialise (the financial sector in London; engineering in the English midlands; textiles in Northern Ireland), creating the possibility of what economists call 'asymmetric' shocks. The regions of the UK can have very different trading relations with other regions and with the rest of the world. For example, the North is more heavily oriented towards the South than is any other UK region. Regional labour markets differ in their degree of 'flexibility' and in the mobility and skills of the labour force. Finally, national fiscal and monetary policies impact differently on regions, with the more prosperous regions of the south of England contributing to the welfare of the less prosperous regions of the north and west of the UK.

Since regional issues appear to be potentially significant, and since there are likely to be regional winners and losers in EMU (whether or not the UK eventually joins), what is the broad context of regional policy? The advent of the Single European Market has already greatly restricted national policy autonomy. EMU simply continues this trend, and some countries like this more than others! However, regions have begun to emerge as 'natural economic zones', which can be regions within a single nation state as well as zones of cross-border co-operation between regions in different nation states. Purely region-specific policies (in the industrial, educational and social spheres) tend to operate on the supply-side of the regional economy. With recent moves towards more regional devolution within the UK, the optimum degree of regional policy autonomy has become a live issue and debate, particularly in Scotland. And finally, since regions will always have a lesser degree of formal policy autonomy than the nation as a whole, there is need for innovative regional mixtures of public and private sector initiatives and collaboration that are perfectly compatible with being an integral part of a nation state.

As a peripheral region of the UK, there are effectively two 'domestic' markets for Northern Ireland to trade in: its own local market and the wider British market. Exchange rate fluctuations will not directly affect Northern Ireland's intra-UK relationship. However, there are indirect factors to be considered which will impact differently on the local and the national economy. Thus, the high sterling rate against the euro has made UK-produced goods less competitive in the domestic UK market to the extent that there are euro-priced competing goods in that market. Since many Northern-produced goods appear to be sold as intermediate inputs to other British firms before being exported as final goods, the North's crucial intra-UK trade is unlikely to be protected for long from sterling's strength against the euro. Of course, the opposite would hold if sterling were to weaken against the euro. This is a serious matter for the North since about 80 per cent of manufacturing employment is domestically (or UK) oriented.

We conclude with some remarks on the effect of EMU on North-South economic interactions. The peace process that emerged during this decade, and that has culminated in the Good Friday Agreement, has been associated with rapid growth and deepening of North-South business and economic ties. The mutually beneficial nature of these developments is widely acknowledged, even if there are different priorities and agendas for future progress. The key question at issue for the immediate future is whether the non-participation of the UK in EMU will erect barriers to increased North-South interactions in the economic and business sphere. We can illustrate just one small aspect of this issue by drawing attention to the finding that small firms in Northern Ireland (i.e. with a turnover of less than £500,000 in 1990 or employing less than 50 people) who sell outside the UK do so predominantly to the Republic of Ireland. Given their characteristics, such firms are also most at risk of EMU-induced loss of competitiveness should sterling strengthen relative to the Euro. Indeed, they are already suffering in this way.

With the UK out of EMU, the North-South border will take on the role of a European policy 'fault line'. Just as with geological fault lines, policy fault lines are going to make it more difficult to encourage the deepening of North-South linkages and structures, and will continue to distort the vulnerable and underdeveloped economies of the immediate cross-border region. More generally, Northern Ireland will be buffeted in the backwash of the consequences of UK non-participation in EMU. In the Republic of Ireland, these negative consequences will tend to be offset by other positive benefits of EMU membership.

The island economy of the future

Industry in Northern Ireland has yet to develop dynamic, self-sustaining characteristics, especially in terms of clusters of related and supporting industries. It remains heavily subsidised by public funding and is concentrated in the low technology sectors of traditional industries such as textiles and clothing. The situation in the South is somewhat healthier, but because industrial development has been so heavily driven by foreign direct investment, which tends not to lay down the full range of developmental roots in the domestic economy, the key interconnections between related firms and industries have yet to take place fully.

How might this situation be improved? Both regions are individually small, with populations of only 1.6 and 3.8 million respectively. The North is not only separated geographically from Britain, but, importantly, also appears to be very weakly integrated into the supply side of the British economy, even when demand for Northern output is driven by the British market. For example, the North is almost never central to strategic planning by British firms and is, therefore, both geographically and economically peripheral to Britain. Recent improvements in access transport and a more positive political situation should help to alleviate this situation over time. But the North is unlikely ever to be placed on a par with the rest of the British economy, at least from the supply side perspective. Rather, it is likely to remain the case that the North will remain economically peripheral to Britain. In contrast, however, there is less geographical or economic logic to the North remaining peripheral to the South.

The logic in favour of deepening North-South supply-side links, thus making the two Irish regions less peripheral to each other, is partly economic (dealing with cross-border policy externalities and spillovers), partly geographic (close proximity and land borders have a unique and inescapable logic of their own), partly cultural (although this aspect is not without problems), and partly political (since deeper North-South economic links might aid the consolidation of peace and political stability within the North and greater North-South trust and harmony).

The situation in the South, relative to the countries that provide the bulk of its foreign direct investment (predominantly the US, but also

Britain and the rest of the EU), has strong analogies with the position in the North. For example, just as the North is not strategically central to externally owned (mainly British) firms located in Northern Ireland, the economy of the South is not central to the strategic planning of many of the (mainly US-based) firms located there. Rather, the South is seen as a highly profitable location for production of products mainly designed, developed, tested and marketed elsewhere, and a location where a very high quality labour force is available at reasonable cost. As already argued, the branch plant nature of foreign firms located in the South does not always encourage the establishment of strong economic performance built on competitive advantage. Heavy dependence on foreign investment is less likely to generate the type of cumulative self-sustaining indigenous growth that is a characteristic of successful European regional economies such as Emilia-Romagna in northern Italy and Baden-Württemberg in Germany.

The Harvard-based business strategist Michael Porter has suggested that four interacting characteristics are essential for competitive success: factor conditions, demand conditions, related and supporting industries, and firm strategy, structure and rivalry. With regard to *factor conditions*, there is clearly much that could be done to improve the level and quality of education, training, infrastructure and technology on an island basis, in much the same way as the South has managed to do over the past decade by itself. As Porter emphasises, improved factor conditions do not come about automatically, but as the result of government and companies bringing them about and subsequently sustaining them.

Demand conditions are a clear example of how island-based activity and policy could bring significant economic improvement. What is required is the creation of sophisticated and demanding local buyers who put pressure on companies to meet high standards in terms of product quality, features and services. There is clearly substantial scope for development on this front, even in the South where industrial success is still tightly focused around the activities of multi-national companies. There seems to be some evidence that foreign plants are beginning to source more inputs locally and that indigenous industry is responding to the challenges that they provide. However, there is certainly potential for further development. The turnaround in performance, documented by ESRI economist Eoin O'Malley, and the increased cross-border trading activity of Northern small and medium-sized businesses suggest that circumstances are already changing for the better.

The third determinant of the competitiveness diamond is the need for *related and supporting industries*. In effect, this is the complement of demand conditions and involves the development of a critical mass of competitive suppliers of specialised components, machinery and services. The relevance of the island economy is that Porter emphasises the importance of geographic proximity and close working relationships for the promotion of the key issue of innovation, involving information flows, technical interchange and the opportunities that exist for sharing. It is in this respect that he presents the case for the importance of *clusters* of related industrial activity, with strong forwards and backwards linkages, both within and between industries.

Fourth is the importance of *firm strategy, structure and rivalry*. Again, the two economies, North and South, would still seem to lack much of what Porter argues for in this regard. For example, he states that companies rarely succeed abroad unless there is intense competitive rivalry at home. In the North, competition is limited and cushioned by high levels of public subsidisation. In the South, foreign industry does not compete locally and indigenous industry, at least until recently, operated in partially sheltered markets due to the element of non-traded goods being produced for home consumption. Intra-island trade on the island has increased in recent years, but there again remains substantial scope for further growth of high technology two-way trade.

What is required to upgrade the four Porter competitiveness factors on the island is not for the North and South to develop separately, as two separate and competing regions, but to come closer together, building on strengths and eradicating weaknesses so that genuine synergies can be realised for the mutual benefit of both North and South. Such synergies would ultimately be reflected in the formation and development of deeply embedded, inter-connected and supportive island industrial activity. This would be seen in the emergence of industrial *clusters* of firms and industries feeding backwards and forwards off each other, industrial *districts* centred around specific industries in specific geographic regions and with the potential to increase local sourcing, and industrial *networks* involving the exchange between firms and industries of mutually-supportive information and knowledge.

The unfortunate reality, as we have already argued, is that both North and South have attempted to improve their competitive advantages in isolation from each other. Given the political climate of the last few decades, this process of separate development is easy to

understand. The type of public and private sector planning and consul-
tation needed to build a Porter-type strategy would have demanded
levels of co-operation that were never realistically going to be politically feasible as long as the conflict in the North continued. However,
the changing and more positive political situation offers many opportunities for development, which to a large degree are already being
taken by the business sectors, through the CBI in the North and IBEC
in the South.

Conclusion

The Northern and Southern economies face very different challenges
in the years ahead. For the North these could be summarised as
follows. There is the question as to how big the 'peace dividend' is
likely to be and how it will affect the structure and performance of the
economy. There is a need for economic restructuring, involving
expansion of the private sector (manufacturing, market services and
agriculture) and shrinking the public sector (at least as a share of the
total economy). Within manufacturing there is also a need for restructuring, involving growth of the modern high technology sectors and
reducing dependence on the traditional sectors, particularly textiles.
After three decades of violent conflict, labour markets have become
segmented both geographically and along religious lines. The result
has been the perpetuation of differential unemployment rates
regionally and between the two main communities.

A series of rather different challenges faces the South. There is a
need to address capacity constraints (particularly in the labour and
housing markets) after an extended period of fast growth. It would be

prudent to try to balance the dependency on foreign direct investment with growth in the indigenous sector to ensure the continued success of the Irish economy as part of the global economy. It is also necessary to proceed rapidly with deregulation of public utilities (telecoms, electricity, etc.) to ensure lower costs to the exposed trading sectors of the economy. Finally, there is a need to address regional imbalances and problems associated with the relatively poor performance of the immediate cross-border areas.

As policy-makers North and South face these challenges, the progressive centralisation of macroeconomic and monetary policy-making in Brussels and Frankfurt will result in a greater focus on the differential performance of regional rather than national economies within the EU. The difference between national success and failure will come to depend increasingly on the ability of regional economies to mobilise their resources and policy-making powers to improve their competitive performance. Regions that do not already have such devolved powers within their own nation states, or who do not seek them, are likely to be at a severe handicap relative to regions that have extensive devolved or federal policy-making structures and are prepared to use them wisely and creatively.

In terms of decreasing importance, the following are the main forces driving economic growth and development, North and South. First, the continuation of peace and the full implementation and operation of the new institutions that arose from the political settlement. Will peace unleash the suppressed potential for faster growth or merely prevent further decline? Second, the need to continue to embrace globalisation and economic openness. Third, the search for locally focused policies to improve the level of human capital and physical infrastructure. Fourth, developments in the local policy-making environment concerning increased autonomy (in the case of Northern Ireland) and progressive ceding of authority to EU institutions (in the cases of the UK and the Republic of Ireland)

The goal in both regions is to raise the level of GDP or GNP per head, thereby increasing local standards of living. In the words of the First Minister, David Trimble, speaking about Northern Ireland: 'The key task is to develop a stronger core of highly productive firms which can support a high standard of living for all of our people. In the long term we would wish this to become self-sustaining, requiring only modest levels of subsidy.'

In identifying different options for economic governance we have paid particular attention to one aspect of the problem: namely, the nature of North-South relationships. In doing so, we are suggesting that the North-South axis is as important as another obvious alternative, namely the East-West axis. A concentration on a North-South axis is perfectly consistent with the fact that the major external markets and sources of inward investment for both regions presently lie, and will continue to lie, outside the island. It is also consistent with the fact that even in the hypothetical situation of a single economy on the island, it would still be one of the most open economies in the world. But openness in terms of trade, in a situation where island production is dominated by foreign multi-national branch plants, is not a position of strength.

We suggest that resolution of economic problems on the North-South axis may be a necessary condition for encouraging growth of strong indigenous firms, including Irish multi-nationals. The separate Southern market of 3.8 million consumers, and the Northern market of 1.6 million, are probably too small to be able to nurture and encourage any high level of local entrepreneurship in isolation from each other. In addition, Northern policy-makers lack the required degree of policy autonomy to compete on an equal footing with Southern initiatives such as the low rate of corporation tax, and are further disadvantaged because of their peripherality within the wider UK market. Perhaps this dilemma could be termed Northern Ireland's 'Southern' problem. To put it very bluntly, the North needs the South more than the South needs the North.

Another misunderstanding of the idea of a island economy is that, quite literally, it seems to advocate an inward-looking insularity. However, Sir George Quigley's characterisation of the island economy challenges us to widen our understanding of the role of small regions and small states in the increasingly integrated global economy. The Japanese business strategist, Kenichi Ohmae, wrote: 'Economic activity is what defines the landscape on which all other institutions, including political institutions, must operate' (Ohmae, 1996).

On the global economic map, the lines that now matter are those defining 'natural economic zones', that represent no threat to the political borders of any nation. The defining issue is that each such zone possesses, in one or other combination, the key ingredients for successful participation in the global economy. Far from advocating insularity, this is effective and relevant global thinking.

Acknowledgements

I acknowledge the collaboration with Douglas Hamilton, who has worked with me on North-South issues for many years, and I have adapted some of our joint work for this study. Michael D'Arcy and Professor Noel Farley of Bryn Mawr College have both been sources of information, criticism and encouragement over the years at times when the prospects for North-South co-operation looked far less promising than they do today. Earlier versions of the present study were presented at seminars held at the Economic and Social Research Institute in Dublin, at Nuffield College, Oxford, and at various other lectures over the years at which I received many useful critical comments and suggestions from colleagues and friends.

Some of the research reported in this study was supported financially during 1998-99 under Measure 3.1 (Cross-Border Business Linkages) of the EU Special Support Programme for Peace and Reconciliation, administered by Co-operation Ireland, and earlier by the International Fund for Ireland. The study also draws on earlier work carried out for the Northern Ireland Economic Council.

The Island Economy:
A Meaningful Concept?

ESMOND BIRNIE

Introduction

This essay seeks to ascertain to what extent, if at all, the concept of an island economy is a meaningful one for Northern Ireland and the Republic of Ireland. In the first part it is asked how far the economic model provided by the Celtic Tiger could be transferred to Northern Ireland. The second section benchmarks the extent of co-operation which has already occurred. The third part critically evaluates the assertion that North-South trade is less than would be reasonably expected. Fourthly, I consider how far a change in the institutional relationship between Northern Ireland and the Republic of Ireland is necessary for the better functioning of the economies. The likely impact of the euro is discussed in the fifth section. Whether Northern Ireland firms should concentrate on the Great Britain or Republic of Ireland markets is considered in the final section.

What, if anything, can Northern Ireland learn from the Celtic Tiger?

The popularity of particular national economic models has often been as short-lived as the fashions demonstrated by the other sort of model. This suggests the need for caution when it comes to using the Republic of Ireland (ROI) economy as a model for Northern Ireland (NI). In the late 1980s, for example, there was a current of American 'declinism' regarding US growth rates and manufacturing performance relative to other Western economies which has since been replaced by an emphasis on the USA's success in terms of entrepreneurship and information technology. In the early 1990s the mood changed to one of 'Eurosclerosis'. The economies of the European Community (later European Union) were perceived as lacking sufficient industrial and labour market flexibility.[1]

As an economics undergraduate student in the mid 1980s I was warned not to pay too much heed to prophecies of doom regarding the end of the Swedish model. It does now seem that the Scandinavian model has gone out of favour. Similarly, the 1990s saw a dimming of enthusiasm for the German and Italian approaches to economic management. Hopefully, assessment of the East Asian tigers has perhaps moved from euphoria through anguish to a more sober evaluation. For all its continuing strengths, the Japanese economy, at the start of the 2000s, remains under a cloud of financial uncertainty and macroeconomic mismanagement.

Given this background, perhaps even the very concept of an exemplary economy needs to be handled with care. When we consider Northern Ireland relative to the Republic of Ireland we need first to assess the explanations of the Celtic Tiger phenomenon and then to evaluate how far these explanatory factors could be transferred to Northern Ireland. With hindsight, the development of the Celtic Tiger since the late 1980s is not surprising, but it did surprise observers at the time.

From the vantage point of 1990 this author would not have forecast that the Republic of Ireland was going to attain at least a decade of economic growth rates above 5 per cent per annum. My only comfort is that my failure places me in distinguished company. There seems to have been no recognition in the late 1980s-early 1990s that the previous trend in Republic of Ireland growth was being replaced with a new, much higher growth path. Observers at that time were agreed that the Republic's long run performance had, at best, fallen short of potential or, at worst, was a dismal disappointment.[2]

At the time of writing there is a developing consensus as to the various factors which have caused the upsurge in Republic of Ireland growth rates. It is possible to consider these in turn to assess the extent to which they might also apply to Northern Ireland.

Demography

The rapid decline in the Republic of Ireland's birth rate since the 1970s implies that the Republic's dependency ratio (i.e. the 'dependent' population of the young and old relative to that population within the working ages) has been dropping and is now much lower than that of most Western economies. These structural changes account for some of the improvement in the Republic of Ireland's level of Gross Domestic Product (GDP) per capita relative to the rest of the EU. This factor represents a once-off gain to living standards and is not likely to be transferable to Northern Ireland. It is true that Northern Ireland's birth rate now lies above that of the Republic. While that rate will almost certainly decline, any gain in terms of a reduction in the proportion of the population aged less than 16 will be more than compensated for by the continuing rapid proportional increase of those in the older age groups.

EU funds

There is no doubt (especially when the impact of the Common Agricultural Policy is included) that the Republic of Ireland has derived substantial benefit in terms of transfers from the EU and to a much greater extent than Northern Ireland.[3] EU transfers may explain about 0.5 percentage points out of ROI growth rates of over 5 per cent since the late 1980s. Northern Ireland is never likely to receive EU subsidy on the same scale as the Republic. In fact Northern Ireland is now entering a period of transition out of Objective One Status and therefore smaller EU funds are available during 2000-2006 than was the case during 1989-2000.

Schooling and education

The Republic of Ireland introduced mass, public-funded upper secondary education in the mid 1960s, about two decades later than most of the rest of north-west Europe. The economy has therefore benefited from the upgrading of its stock of human capital but much later than in many of the EU economies. In fact those dividends were being reaped in the late 1980s when the turnaround in the Republic's growth began. This human capital improvement is a once-off gain[4] and therefore not one which Northern Ireland can repeat. It is possible that the Republic made some clever policy moves, and Northern Ireland could learn from these, in terms of technical education and further and higher education (e.g. the Regional Technical Colleges, as they used to be called) but this remains unclear.

Catch-up

This point is similar to that relating to schooling. The Republic of Ireland in the late 1980s was starting from a relatively low base in terms of levels of GDP per head. It therefore had scope for relatively easy growth by imitation of those economies at the frontiers of technological practice.[5] Northern Ireland in the first decade of the new century starts from a higher comparative position (relative to the United Kingdom or the EU average in per capita GDP terms) than that occupied by the Republic in the late 1980s. There is therefore less scope for catch-up though there is some.

R and D and physical capital

Most exercises in international growth accounting have attributed a significant component of growth to research and development (R and D) and physical capital expenditures. The recent experience of the Republic of Ireland is somewhat unusual since neither of these factors seem to have been a significant cause of its growth during 1988-2000. R and D levels have begun to increase but still remain low by EU standards (though they have surpassed the very low levels in Northern Ireland). The Republic's current National Development Plan (2000-2006) does envisage enormous improvements in the physical infrastructure (e.g. roads, railways, sewerage, telecoms and housing). However, these changes are more the fruit of the Celtic Tiger phenomenon than its cause.

Copying from better practice in policy making

Could Northern Ireland learn from recent policy initiatives and institutional developments in the Republic of Ireland? Perhaps it could do so with special attention being paid to the areas of social partnership and industrial development policy.

Social partnership

With respect to social partnership it may well be significant that the Republic has moved away from the decentralised UK style of wage bargaining and towards a more centralised, corporatist/tripartite or 'continental' model. (However there are limits as to how far the Republic has moved towards the European labour market model. These were illustrated by the recent comments of the *Tanaiste* [deputy prime minister], Mary Harney, that Ireland is 'spiritually closer to Boston than Berlin. Our economic success owes more to American liberalism than to European leftism'.)

At the time of writing in autumn 2000 this ROI model was straining to contain hitherto repressed wage inflation. In September 2000 the headline inflation rate reached 6.2 per cent and the President of the European Central Bank, Wim Duisenberg, grimly predicted: 'Economies like the Netherlands and Ireland are experiencing a little bit of a free ride which cannot last forever.' That said, for over a decade the rate of wage increase has been much lower than the growth of productivity. In consequence there has been a redistribution of national income towards profits. This is part and parcel of an industrial development policy which has relied very heavily on the attraction of inward investment. How far the relative squeeze on wages contributed to Celtic Tiger growth remains unclear. It is very doubtful if Northern Ireland could remain part of the UK economy and yet decouple from the UK approach to wage bargaining so as either to go it alone or to hook up to the Republic.

Industrial development policy

In March 1999 the administration in Northern Ireland introduced the economic strategy document *Strategy 2010*. Less than a year later the main industrial development agency (Forfás) in the Republic published *Enterprise 2010*. This coincidence of timing makes it very appropriate to consider both the similarities and contrasts between Northern and Southern industrial development policies.

The review of policy in NI was instigated by the Department of Economic Development (DED).[6] The DED and its successor, the Department of Enterprise, Trade and Investment (DETI), act as an umbrella organisation covering a range of industrial development agencies.[7] The process of construction of *Strategy 2010* during February 1998-March 1999 made use of 18 working groups totalling about 300 people who were drawn partly from the private sector. In practice, however, the final document was heavily weighted towards the 'insider' official view on industrial policy.[8] This would certainly be suggested by the composition of the steering group responsible for *Strategy 2010*, where only six out of the 13 members could readily be described as private sector and where the chairman also happened to be the Permanent Secretary of the Department whose policy was under review.[9]

In the Republic of Ireland, *Enterprise 2010* was promoted by the Forfás agency whose responsibilities for enterprise development, technology and innovation make it broadly comparable to the Department of Economic Development.[10] In this case also the steering committee of the new strategy was heavily weighted towards the public sector. One difference, which may have been significant, was that this committee of 15 contained at least three persons with direct experience of economic research whereas in Northern Ireland such experience was largely absent. Gillespie claims that far from the latter factor being a weakness, it was actually a strength, because the DED was thereby able to benefit from input which was very much anchored in local experience and business orientated rather than being an 'abstract economic thesis'.

At the level of aspirations there is a lot of similarity between NI and the Republic. *Strategy 2010* outlines the need for a 'fast growing, competitive, innovative, knowledge-based economy where there are plentiful opportunities and a population equipped to grasp them'. Similarly *Enterprise 2010* says that 'Ireland has within its grasp the capacity to achieve a quality of life for all its citizens which is among the highest and most widely-shared in the developed world'.

In both NI and the Republic there is a strong optimism that a trade-off between equity and efficiency can be avoided. In other words, it can be possible to tackle hard core poverty or 'social exclusion' while at the same time maintaining high growth rates. Time will tell if such optimism is warranted. However, Callan and Nolan have showed that the level of inequality was stable between the mid 1980s and the mid 1990s in the Republic of Ireland while it rose in the UK (separate data for NI are not available). They also demonstrated that the increase in female participation in the ROI was not, unlike that in the UK and USA, accompanied by increased inequality.

The Northern Ireland Economic Council has been forthright in criticising the *Strategy 2010* for its lack of a worked-out economic model.

By this they did not mean a fully specified regional econometric model, but rather some view, even if somewhat informal, as to what benchmark performance would have been in the absence of the policy proposals, together with some view as to the connections between chosen policy instruments and desired outcomes. The Council argued that the absence of such a model implied there was a low probability that *Strategy 2010* would hit the policy objectives which have been identified. Moreover, in the absence of a model, it would be difficult to say whether policy was having an impact.

In the case of the Republic the model could be labelled 'the USA competitiveness model' (i.e. one attributable to Porter and the various late-1980s enquiries into American industrial competitiveness). The OECD's definition of competitiveness is favoured, i.e. a region or country is competitive if it can maintain or expand its market share in free international markets while also increasing the per capita income of its people in the long run. This approach to competitiveness now also governs policy in Great Britain as shown by, for example, the creation of the Competitiveness Council in 1999.

In this scheme of things, pride of place is given to raising the level and growth rate of labour productivity as a means towards maximising competitiveness. It involves the building up and maintenance of a world-class standard traded goods and services sector. In this respect the Republic has the advantage, relative to Northern Ireland, that it can now build on the considerable achievement of the last decade or so. Republic of Ireland manufacturing labour productivity levels now appear to be higher than those in the UK, even after correction for the transfer pricing distortions introduced by the multi-nationals.

Moreover, and here there is a contrast to the East Asian tiger economies during their phase of catch-up, the Republic's total factor productivity growth has been strong. (Total factor productivity is what is left unexplained after as much growth as possible has been explained by other factors, notably growth in employment and the physical capital stock.) Hence its GDP growth cannot simply be attributed to additions to the combined input of capital and labour. However it is also true that while total factor productivity growth has been respectable, ROI labour productivity growth has been more mundane.

Enterprise 2010 indicates that the Republic of Ireland's long term, sustainable rate of growth of Gross National Product (GNP) could and should be 5 per cent per annum. This depends on raising GNP per head growth rates to 3 per cent per annum (about 0.5 per cent per annum higher than the trend rate in the first half of the 1990s) alongside annual employment growth rates of 2 per cent (lower than the bumper annual employment growth rates above 4 per cent experienced in the late 1990s, but still much higher than the trend for recent decades and also very high by Western economy standards).

Both strategy documents aim high. In the Republic it is anticipated that both GDP and GNP per capita will be substantially higher than the EU (15 countries) average ten years from now. Considering the lower base from which it must start, *Strategy 2010* in Northern Ireland is also quite demanding in that it suggests GDP per capita should increase from its current level of about four-fifths of the UK average up to 90 per cent by 2010.

Both documents include a number of statistical indicators, notably on the levels of R and D as percentages of GDP. However given that the Republic's document has been more explicit in highlighting a US-style productivity and competitiveness model, it can integrate such targets throughout the various parts of the strategy in a more coherent and credible manner.

Given the similarity between the two strategies in terms of their timing and ultimate objectives, it is interesting to evaluate their prospects of success. The conclusion must be that the Republic's strategy is more likely to be successful than its Northern Ireland counterpart.[11] This is partly because it takes place against a background of very considerable economic success. Indeed, it is possible that into the medium term future the Republic's economy will continue to record a substantial rate of economic growth almost regardless of the type of industrial policy which is adopted. What *Enterprise 2010* does have in its favour is an explicit economic model and/or theory underlying the policy recommendations. Moreover, the Republic's strategy will be delivered within the context of a relatively settled political and administrative structure.

The Northern Ireland strategy lacks these advantages. Northern Ireland may well have out-performed the average level of UK macroeconomic performance throughout the 1990s, although not by a large enough margin to prove that a powerful underlying and sustained process of convergence (in terms of productivity, living standards, and structure of the economy) has occurred. Whereas the Republic's strategy can tap into the largesse available from a cash-rich national exchequer,[12] the NI strategy takes place against the background of relatively tightly constrained UK public expenditure. *Strategy 2010* lacks a model of the regional economy or any well thought-out view of the transmission mechanisms connecting policy measures and final policy objectives. Moreover, at least at the time of writing, the viability and stability of the political structures within Northern Ireland remain uncertain.[13]

Strategy 2010 is something of a wish list of desirable characteristics for a regional economy (there are 62 numbered policy recommendations), which does not prioritise between these objectives and gives little appreciation of how scarce resources are to be mobilised and allocated. The Northern Ireland strategy fails to address the central and chronic deficiency of the regional economy: a lack of competitiveness in the tradeables sectors. In this respect *Strategy 2010* differs from *Enterprise 2010* which does give a central focus to raising sectoral productivity. This implies that Northern Ireland does have some scope to learn from the Republic's current industrial development strategy.

Economic development policy more generally

The influential work of Michael Porter has popularised notions of competitive advantage, be they of city, region, or country. His approach could encourage a shopping list approach to improving competitiveness (e.g. 'If we copy the following ten features of the Baden-Württemburg economy then we will surely imitate its performance'). This was probably not Porter's intention. In truth, regions and countries often attain competitive advantage precisely because they are doing something which no one else is doing. This, once again, makes it unlikely that it is a matter of Northern Ireland following along the same path already taken by the Republic of Ireland.

The Republic may well have done something interesting with respect to promoting skills and facilitating private (and foreign)

LYIT
LIBRARY
LETTERKENNY

investment in growth sectors. Northern Ireland policy-makers can and should learn something from this, but what they learn is hardly earth-shattering. It is probably true that successive governments in the Republic since 1987 have produced a context within which other factors (favourable demographic change, assistance from the EU, dividends from previous upgrading of human capital and scope for catch-up) produced a favourable break in the trend of growth. Like doctors, governments and managers of the economy should do no harm. It would seem that for a decade and a half governments in the Republic have largely done no harm. This is a valuable example to their counterparts in Northern Ireland.

Previous policy measures to promote Co-operation between Northern Ireland and the Republic of Ireland

The nature and extent of economic links between Northern Ireland and the Republic of Ireland have probably been given more attention than any other type of link between Northern Ireland and the rest of the world. In one sense this is surprising, given that NI remains a UK regional economy highly integrated within that national economy. However, the creation of institutions to promote increased North-South economic co-operation has sometimes been viewed as an essential component in an overall political settlement in Northern Ireland, and this has been official Anglo-Irish policy from the 1995 Frameworks Document through to the 'three strand' multi-party Belfast Agreement (better known as the Good Friday Agreement) of April 1998.

A striking feature of the political economy of North-South co-operation in the mid to late 1990s is the number of parallels to developments about forty years previously. The then Republic of Ireland Minister for Industry and Commerce, Seán Lemass, declared in 1959: 'Ireland is too small a country not to be seriously handicapped in its economic development by its division into two areas separated by a customs barrier.' During 1958-65, as forty years later, there was a tension between the anti-partitionist rhetoric of the Dublin government and its fear that all-Ireland arrangements might harm the Republic's economic interests. The unionist leadership, for its part, often feared economic co-operation as a Trojan horse for constitutional change, but in practice was prepared to be pragmatic given pressure from the Northern Ireland business community.[14] In contemporary debates it has been claimed that the current level of integration is less than would be reasonably expected, and therefore there would be larger gains to both Irish economies through ever-increasing integration. This essay will outline the kinds of co-operation which were already in place by the end of the 1990s, before considering the above assertions.

The main area of policy intervention aimed at promoting cross-border economic integration has been with respect to industry and trade. The Confederation of British Industry and the Confederation of Irish Industry (later the Irish Business and Employers Confederation) have been working jointly at a sectoral level to identify opportunities for greater trade for nearly a decade. Chambers of commerce in the two jurisdictions have also sponsored schemes to promote cross-border trade. Development agencies have attempted to encourage local sourcing (e.g. by the multi-national plants) on an all-Ireland basis. There has also been some pooling of research activities in the universities. Some of these links were reflected in the programme of the North-South Trade and Business Development Body which came into being in December 1999 as one of the North-South 'implementation bodies' set up under the terms of the Good Friday Agreement.

Agriculture, fishing and forestry provide examples of some longstanding and successful North-South initiatives. For example, since 1952 there has been common management of the Foyle Fisheries together with reciprocal fishing rights in coastal waters (which is of mutual benefit given the NI specialism in shellfish and that of the Republic in whitefish). Animal health programmes have also been run in parallel. There were difficulties, however, in the 1980s as divergent exchange rate movements and the consequent differences in prices to farmers provided incentives for disruptive and variable movements of animals across the border. (One consequence of the 1996-98 BSE crisis was that the Republic sealed its border to prevent the movement of cattle from Northern Ireland to its processing plants.) A North-South food safety 'implementation body' was set up in 1999. Under the Good Friday Agreement, agriculture represents an area for enhanced co-operation between the existing Departments and agencies.

There are a number of institutional links between the financial systems in the two economies. However, the breaking of the Irish pound-pound sterling parity in 1978 and the subsequent variation of the Republic of Ireland/UK exchange rate has made co-operation more difficult. This will be all the more so if, as now seems almost inevitable, the Republic of Ireland is among the first group of members of a new European single currency, while the UK decides to opt out for at least a couple of years.

The regulatory regime in Northern Ireland since 1979 has probably moved further away from that in the Republic. Both economies have a stock exchange but the Belfast exchange does not perform a capital-raising function. Ironically, Republic of Ireland firms, through their use of the Dublin stock exchange, may now be more integrated into the London stock exchange. Certainly the Republic's economy now has proportionately more (and much larger) home-grown PLCs than exist in Northern Ireland.

At the start of the 1990s 8 per cent of the Republic's out-of-state tourist revenue derived from visitors from the North, while Southern visitors to Northern Ireland represented 17 per cent of total tourist revenues there. Thus cross-border tourist flows were especially important to the Northern Ireland economy. There is already co-operation in terms of joint marketing and booking facilities and these were upgraded in late 1996. A joint tourist promotion company (with the two tourist authorities as principal shareholders) is due to be formed in the near future.

In the early 1970s there was a 300 MW electricity interconnection which probably yielded a total benefit of IR£10 million annually in terms of pooling generation capacity and lowering the marginal cost of supply. Repeated terrorist attacks brought an end to this form of co-operation, which was re-instated after the 1994 ceasefires. The main North-South interconnector was put back in place in March 1995 at a cost of £1.2 m. to Northern Ireland Electricity and £400,000 to the ESB.

The savings to each system are £500,000 annually. It has been reckoned that in the long run annual capacity savings would be one per cent of total Irish electricity generating costs. A number of standby links between the electricity supply in the north west of Northern Ireland and the Donegal-Sligo region have always been maintained and the feasibility of interconnection of gas supplies is being considered.

A number of formal and informal links exist in the area of transport such as the joint operation of the Dublin-Belfast railway. Northern firms use the ports of Rosslare and Waterford and Southern firms use Larne and Warrenpoint.

All this represents a mass of initiatives which seek to promote economic co-operation. They differ in the way in which government is involved. Some schemes are sponsored by local government, others by semi-state organisations, central government or supranational agencies (mainly the EU). In aggregate the measures are quite small relative to the total size of the economies. They tend to reflect piecemeal reaction to circumstances rather than some grand design. Measures to promote North-South economic co-operation have been allowed to develop in a pragmatic and decentralised way. This may have been the most appropriate approach unless it is thought there was some alternative which would have generated larger benefits.

The 1998 Good Friday Agreement will probably not herald a quantum leap in the extent of common policy-making and administrative, economic and social integration between the two Irish economies. In contrast, the earlier approach of the two governments as expressed in the 1995 Frameworks Document had ambitious plans for cross-border executive bodies tasked to harmonise policies and economic outcomes and with an internal 'dynamic' with respect to their range of functions. Whilst the early draft agreement from the inter-party talks chairman, Senator George Mitchell, seemed to envisage very extensive powers for all-Ireland political authorities,[15] the final agreement adopted a tentative tone as to which areas of possible co-operation might be placed within the scope of the North/South Ministerial Council.[16] At least six entirely new implementation bodies were to be created (subject to the overall constitutional package being adopted). It appears that the Ulster Unionist negotiators succeeded in their objective of maintaining the principle that any agencies operating at an all-Ireland level should be strictly accountable to the Northern Ireland Assembly.

In December 1998 it was agreed that there would be six implementation bodies and six areas for enhanced co-operation as follows:

North-South Implementation Bodies	Areas for enhanced North-South co-operation
Inland waterways	Transport
Food safety	Agriculture
Trade and business development	Education
Special EU programmes	Health
Language	Environment
Aquaculture and marine matters	Tourism

From a political economy viewpoint, an interesting question is why certain implementation bodies were included and others were not. For example, the inclusion of language implies that cultural issues weighed more heavily with some on the nationalist-republican side of the negotiations than economic ones.[17] Conversely, whereas there might have appeared to be some scope for co-operation in the fields of transport and energy, neither was included in the final list of six bodies (energy was not even in the areas for enhanced co-operation through existing institutions, notwithstanding the cross-border implications of implementing EU Directives on liberalising electricity markets).

Is the level of North-South trade and economic interchange abnormally low?

This is a crucial question. Increased trade and economic interchange are, other things being equal, good things. However, to the extent that they are promoted through the outlay of public money there will be a opportunity cost. We need to find out the socially optimal level of trade and interchange and (by implication) whether current performance falls short of that ideal. The question is also begged (though it is rarely addressed in the literature in this area) as to why, if increased trade and interchange are so self-evidently desirable, these outcomes do not happen anyway without any appeal for policy intervention.

Table 1 attempts to summarise the recent trading performance of the Northern Ireland economy by presenting estimates of the geographical composition of manufacturing sales during the 1990s.

Table 1: Northern Ireland Manufacturing Sector:
Total Sales, External Sales and Exports

(£ million, current prices) (Percentage composition of sales in parenthesis)

	1991/92 (%)		1995/96 (%)		1998/99 (%)	
Total sales	6450	(100)	8705	(100)	9261	(100)
Northern Ireland	2278	(35)	2826	(32)	2702	(29)
External sales	4172	(65)	5879	(68)	6559	(71)
Great Britain	2388	(37)	2806	(32)	3166	(34)
Export sales	1784	(28)	3073	(35)	3393	(37)
Republic of Ireland	437	(7)	710	(8)	792	(9)
Rest of EU	786	(12)	1242	(14)	1052	(11)
Rest of world	561	(9)	1121	(13)	1549	(14)

Note: These estimates were constructed using a variety of sources. The principal source was the Northern Ireland Economic Research Centre (NIERC)'s survey of all manufacturing firms with 20 or more employees. This was augmented by the Annual Survey by the small firms agency LEDU. To account for any under-representation of small firms, a number of small non-assisted firms with fewer than 20 employees were also surveyed. Overall coverage in the manufacturing sector is high, accounting for approximately 90 per cent of manufacturing employment in 1995/96 and about 45 per cent of manufacturing firms. Estimates for all manufacturing firms are produced by grossing up by sector and size range. *Sources: NIERC, DED, LEDU (1997, 1999).*

The data shown in Table 2 are restricted to manufacturing but are highly indicative of the overall performance of the Northern Ireland economy. In the early 1990s external sales from manufacturing were over £4 billion, with another £500 million from agriculture and less than this from the other tradeables, such as tourism and financial services.

The total level of external sales increased from about 44 per cent of regional GDP in 1991/92 to 48 per cent in 1995/96 (if it is assumed that non-manufacturing external sales increased from £700 million to £800 million during that period). Exports properly defined - i.e. sales going outside the UK - increased from about 20 to 26 per cent (assuming non-manufacturing exports increased from £400 million to £500 million).

Table 2: Northern Ireland Manufacturing Sales Growth (in nominal terms) 1991/92–1998/99

Geographical destination	Total percentage growth
Total sales	44
Northern Ireland	19
External sales	57
Great Britain	33
Export sales	90
Republic of Ireland	81
Rest of EU	34
Rest of the world	176

Sources: As Table 1.

Throughout the first half of the 1990s the geographical composition of Northern Ireland manufacturing sales remained roughly stable: about one-third were sold within Northern Ireland, one-third to Great Britain and the remaining third were exports to the rest of the world (including the Republic of Ireland). However, as Table 2 shows, during the 1990s sales within Northern Ireland and to Britain increased more slowly than the average for all external sales and exports. In the period 1991/92-1998/99 sales to the Republic of Ireland and expats generally increased at about three times the rate of sales to Great Britain. In part, Northern Ireland was participating in a general EU-wide and indeed global trend whereby rates of growth of international trade were higher than those for Gross Domestic Products. Economies have become more open.

Trade between the two Irish economies provides the most visible manifestation of their inter-relationship and this area has been stressed by those, such as the Confederation of Irish Industry in 1990, who have claimed large benefits from further linkage between the two economies.

Table 3: Trade between Northern Ireland and the Republic of Ireland(cross-border merchandise exports)

| | From NI | | From the ROI | |
| | £ m. | % of GDP | £ m. | % of GDP |
	(current prices)		(current prices)	
1960	7.4	2.4	20.3	3.7
1972	30.9	2.9	66.9	2.9
1991	496.2	4.7	789.5	3.3
1995	678.0	4.9	785.0	1.9
1996	734.0	5.0	822.0	1.8
1997	778.0	5.0	1062.0	2.0
1998	792.0	5.0	1184.0	1.9
1999	891.0	n.a.	1175.0	1.7

Sources: 1960-91: Simpson (1993). 1995 onwards: trade and GDP data from the CSO (ROI) and the Department of Enterprise, Trade and Investment in Northern Ireland

As Table 3 illustrates, the extent of trade appears small both in absolute terms and relative to the size of the two economies. The table also shows that a Republic of Ireland trade surplus relative to Northern Ireland has been a longstanding feature. (It is worth remembering that there is no good *economic* reason why NI should be expected to have a bilateral trading surplus with the Republic, any more than the USA should, be expected to have a bilateral surplus with, say, Japan.)

In neither economy is the scale of exports within Ireland large relative to total GDP. This conclusion has been reinforced by detailed studies of the export destinations of Northern Ireland manufactured products by the Northern Ireland Economic Research Centre, the Northern Ireland Industrial Development Board and the Department of Economic Development. Of total sales of £6.5 billion in 1991-92, seven per cent went to the Republic of Ireland, while in 1998-99, of total sales of £9.3 billion, nine per cent went to the Republic (see Table 1). However, Scott and O'Reilly cast some doubt on whether the extent of trade integration between Northern Ireland and the Republic of Ireland is lower than would be expected given that both are very small markets within a world or even an EU context. For example, in proportional terms the trade flows between various Scandinavian economies are of a similar size.[18]

As MacEnroe and Poole have noted, in 1991 Northern Ireland sold about £120 of manufactured goods to each person in the Republic of Ireland compared to NI sales of only about £40 per head to Great Britain, meaning that at least on this measure there was already stronger trade integration between the two Irish economies than there was between Northern Ireland and the rest of the national UK market.

It is thus strange that Michie and Sheehan should feel able to comment that 'the two economies remain poorly integrated'. They go on to qualify, and in fact weaken, this statement by adding 'this reflects the limits of co-operation achievable under two different national jurisdictions, in other words, under current constitutional arrangements'. In other words, their objection to the *status quo* is much more political than economic.

Can there be a successfully co-ordinated Island Economy in two separate political jurisdictions?

The analysis of trade patterns set out above prompts this very interesting question. Some of the theory and practice of European integration since the 1950s might be taken to imply that the answer to this question is 'no'. For example, the development of the Single European Market since the late 1980s has been accompanied by convergence in regulation in the various EU member states. There has been (and may yet be more) centralisation of decision-making through qualified majority voting in the Council of Ministers. Commentators on Northern Ireland-Republic of Ireland links sometimes invoke the theory of neo-functionalism, often applied to the EU, whereby increased co-operation in economic and social matters drives ever-increasing political union. However, it is worth remembering that the European Union is still administered *through* the governments of the member states. The North-South Ministerial Council may not, in any case, be analogous to the EU Council of Ministers.[19] In short, comparisons with the EU may sometimes obscure as much as they clarify.

Much depends on how a 'successfully co-ordinated island economy' is defined. Markets and free(-ish) trade will allocate and co-ordinate in a manner which might be deemed acceptable *if* certain divergences between countries (e.g. in tax rates or levels of regulation) are seen as the expression of differing preferences, as opposed to barriers to competition in need of obliteration through 'upward harmonisation'. Take, for example, environmental policy. Northern Ireland, as part of the UK, has gone some way (through the projected Climate Change Levy) toward carbon taxing. The Republic of Ireland has further to go in this regard. As a consequence, duty on petrol and diesel is considerably higher in the North than in the Republic. This situation, where Northern Ireland enterprises are being put under competitive pressure by their Republic of Ireland counterparts, could prompt one of the following responses:

(a) Northern Ireland should harmonise down to ROI tax rates on energy.

(b) Republic of Ireland should harmonise up to NI tax rates.

(c) Northern Ireland will have to accept some short-term economic and political pain given its fiscal divergence from the Republic. That pain may be rewarded in due course by the long-term social and economic benefits of a more 'green' performance.

Option (a) might appear the easy one in political terms. Bodies like the North-South Ministerial Council could be used to promote option (b). However, is the Republic's policy establishment at all likely to harmonise up to UK regulatory standards on the environment? Similar issues emerge with respect to water quality and waste recycling standards, where again the Republic lags behind the UK, which in turn falls behind best practice in the European Union. Option (c) is a brave and far-sighted one even if it remains politically unpopular, especially in the light of the widespread protests in the summer of 2000 against current levels of UK indirect tax on fuel.

Problems such as the above might appear less pressing if there was a single government and jurisdiction on the island of Ireland. Unsurprisingly, I am not in favour of moving from two separate political jurisdictions. If the Good Friday Agreement means anything, it has enshrined the consent principle relating to the constitutional destiny of Northern Ireland.

Michael Porter makes clear that notwithstanding the impact of so-called globalisation, it still matters what local/regional administrations do. Like many others, I anticipate that the shift from Direct Rule to devolution in Northern Ireland will produce some economic gains. It would seem strange to remove some of these advantages by ill-advised shifts in decision-making up to the all-island level.[20] It is also worth remembering that any administrative economies and advances gained through moving towards increased harmonisation between Northern Ireland and the Republic might be more than outweighed by costs imposed on the NI economy by increased dislocation relative to the rest of the UK.

What would be the role of the Euro?

It is almost certain that the Irish border as a currency frontier between the Pound Sterling and the euro will be entrenched after 2002 (of course that border has been something of a currency frontier since 1978, when the Punt entered the European Monetary System while the Pound Sterling remained outside). The UK's decision whether to join the euro eventually will be made on national considerations, and so the local concerns or needs of Newry, Strabane or Londonderry will not be given much weight. However, even if it were judged that Northern Ireland border areas would gain from membership of the euro, it could still be argued that the province as a whole gets more from being part of the UK (as a complete social, political and economic package) than it loses as a result of that membership.

If the UK (including NI) were in the euro, then the exchange rate risk (i.e. the impact of volatility between currencies) between businesses on the two sides of the Irish border would be zero. This would, other things being equal, give some encouragement to cross-border links. If we look at the likely situation after 2002, it may be that with Republic of Ireland 'in' but the UK 'out', the extent of exchange rate risk between the two countries will be worse than before. This would be because the euro will tend to move in sympathy with continental macroeconomic conditions which are not sychronised with the trade cycle in the UK.[21]

After 2002, firms in the Republic may well find it easier than their Northern Ireland counterparts to trade with the continental EU, given the removal of exchange rate risk. However, it is also possible that the exchange rate risk between the euro and the dollar and far eastern currencies will be higher than that between the pound sterling and those currencies. Northern Ireland's trade to the rest of the world other than the EU is considerable (in 1998–99 £1.5 billion. compared to £1.9 billion). In the 1990s that trade with the rest of the world was increasing very rapidly, and it is possible that after 2002

NI firms will have a competitive advantage relative to the Republic in this huge market.

Should Northern Ireland firms concentrate on British or Southern markets?

In answering this question it might be objected that it is not really a case of 'either/or' when it comes to commercial decisions. Firms can and should allow the market to indicate through profit signals where greater attention should be directed in order to reap the best commercial reward. The dilemma of 'GB versus Republic of Ireland' does become pressing when the public sector intervenes in order to promote trade, investment or economic linkages generally. Such semi-political interventions do not necessarily follow market signals. To the extent that there are pervasive market failures, such interventions might be justified. However, as previous parts of this essay have attempted to indicate, the evidence of systematic market failure in the North-South context is by no means convincing. The intervention which has occurred has been directed almost exclusively towards North-South trading links as opposed to those between Northern Ireland and Great Britain. This weighting probably reflects political factors much more than economic ones.

I want to consider the extent of inter-firm linkages at an all-Ireland level. By global and European standards, firms in either Irish economy are usually relatively small. Does this matter, and could there be large gains through mergers, acquisitions and alliances on an all-Ireland basis? Standard economic theory notes the importance of economies of scale. As output rises the average cost of producing each unit of that output often drops. Could a lack of such economies of scale explain the weak competitiveness performance of Northern Ireland manufacturing? In the early 1990s the average (median by employment) plant size in NI manufacturing was only about 70 per cent of that in Great Britain, and in the Republic of Ireland about 60 per cent. As two small economies, it is not surprising that firms in the two Irish jurisdictions are also generally small, with only a small representation of larger-sized enterprises (those employing more than 499 persons).

However, as Table 4 illustrates, the Republic of Ireland now has a number of companies within the list of Europe's top 500 companies (by market capitalisation) whereas Northern Ireland has none (the origin of a company being determined by the location of its headquarters). Once adjustment is made for relative population size, it would appear that if Northern Ireland had been as successful as the Republic or any of the small continental economies illustrated in the table, then it would have had at least one representative in Europe's top 500. If it had been as successful as either Norway or Switzerland there would have been three.

Table 4 :Development of Large PLCs – Northern Ireland compared to small European economies (number of companies within Europe's top 500 by market capitalisation)

	NI	ROI	Switz.	Belg.	Den.	Swed.	Austr.	Neth.	Nor.
Manufac turing	0	3	5	4	2	6	2	7	5
Nonman- ufacturing	0	0	8	7	3	3	3	4	4
Total	0	3	13	11	5	9	5	11	9
Total if had NI's pop.*	0	1.3	3.1	1.8	1.6	1.7	1.0	1.2	3.4

Note: *Actual total adjusted downwards according to the ratio between the size of that country's population and the population of Northern Ireland.

Source: *The Financial Times* (22 January 1998) 'FT 500 1998'.

Even by the standards of the Republic of Ireland, Northern Ireland's locally controlled manufacturing firms have relatively small turnovers (one of the companies formerly on this list, Shorts, has in recent years become part of an international group, while the previous second ranking company, Powerscreen, collapsed a financial crisis). This is illustrated even more graphically by Table 5.

Table 5: Largest Northern Ireland-controlled
manufacturing firms compared to the Republic's
three largest companies

NI company	Turnover (£m.)*	Sector	ROI (indigenous) company	Turnover (£m.)*
United Dairy Farmers	219.3	Dairying	CRH	4103.9
Desmond and Sons	116.4	Clothing	Jefferson Smurfit	2888.0
Boxmore	106.7	Packaging	Kerry Group	1732.6
Lagan Holding	94.9	Engineering		
Rotary	90.3	Engineering		
O'Kane Poultry	85.2	Meat processing		
Lamont	83.2	Textiles		
Barnett and Hall	86.0	Agri-processing		
John Hogg	78.9	Textiles		
Fane Valley Co-op	78.1	Agri-processing		

Note: *At the market exchange rate. The ROI company sectors are, respectively, materials, packaging and dairying

Source: *Business* (Belfast) *Telegraph* (23 February 2000), 'Northern Ireland's Top 100 Companies'

Table 6 emphasises the much greater penetration of the Northern Ireland private sector by Republic of Ireland owners than *vice versa*.

Table 6: Ownership of the Top 100 Companies
in Northern Ireland and Republic of Ireland,
1994 and *1999 (numbers in italics)*

	Top 50		51-100		Top 100	
Northern Ireland						
Indigenous	22	*14*	34	*22*	56	*36*
Republic of Ireland	9	*7*	7	*4*	16	*11*
UK	13	*16*	5	*14*	18	*30*
USA	2	*5*	2	*7*	4	*12*
Others	4	*8*	2	*3*	6	*11*
Total	50	*50*	50	*50*	100	*100*
Republic of Ireland						
Indigenous	31	*32*	32	*28*	63	*60*
Northern Ireland	0	*0*	0	*0*	0	*0*
UK	5	*4*	3	*4*	8	*8*
USA	9	*13*	8	*16*	17	*29*
Others	5	*1*	7	*2*	12	*3*
Total	50	*50*	50	*50*	100	*100*

Sources: *Ulster Business* (August 1994) 'Top 100' and *Business and Finance* (January 1994)
'Top 1000.' *Belfast Telegraph* (23 February 2000) 'Northern Ireland's Top 100 Companies' and
Business and Finance' Ireland's Top 1000 Companies' (January 2000).

To summarise, the data from tables 4 and 5 could indicate the possibility of gains from increased scale through Northern Ireland
companies merging with, or being acquired by, Republic of Ireland

companies. Table 6 indicates that this process has already started. Such developments might be politically unpalatable to some unionists in Northern Ireland, although this resistance might decline if the April 1998 political agreement does stick.[22] Some of the opposition to increased Southern ownership of Northern Ireland firms would be reduced if there were more takeovers in the opposite direction. In fact, the fears on the Northern side are not simply those of a political nature. There is, for example, a concern that part of the Northern Ireland food processing sector is going to be reduced to the limited role of supplier of raw materials to the much larger enterprises south of the border. The example here is the way in which some of the very big dairy co-ops and plcs in the Republic of Ireland have bought over milk operations in Northern Ireland.

Conclusion

This essay has focused on how far there is an island economy in Ireland. In so doing it has not considered a number of important extra-regional links. For example, there is the question of whether the cost, frequency and reliability of transport connections between Northern Ireland and the rest of the world impedes cost competitiveness (this is probably not as large a negative factor as has often been argued).

Northern Ireland is a region with a history of exporting some of its surplus labour to the rest of the UK (i.e. without net emigration, unemployment rates would have been even higher). More recently, commentators have begun to worry that emigration may erode the region's stock of human capital to the extent that those who leave are the ones with above average levels of qualifications. Differential emigration rates may also go some way to explain the persistent difference between Catholic and Protestant unemployment rates, and may also have long-term implications for voting patterns. There are some connections between the wage rates set in Great Britain and counterpart levels in Northern Ireland, whether through the operation of national wage bargaining or, from 1999 onwards, the national minimum wage.

This essay has considered the overall extent of trading and co-operative links between the two Irish economies. In addition to this there has been a recent debate as to whether there might be large gains to economic integration concentrated in a so-called Belfast-Dublin economic corridor. While strongly competitive clusters or corridors of economic activity do exist in various parts of the Western world, and some of these do cut across frontiers (e.g. Vancouver-Seattle or the Swiss-French-German region around Basle), it is unlikely that the Belfast-Dublin corridor currently displays many of the preconditions which are probably necessary for such developments: world class research and development facilities, a large number of internationally competitive manufacturing firms and a high density of good transport links.

The contents of this contribution can be summarised as follows. Much of the Celtic Tiger phenomenon represents a once and for all economic adjustment. In so far as it is such a once-off adjustment, Northern Ireland cannot imitate the Republic's process of change and economic growth. However, Northern Ireland could learn some valuable policy lessons from the Republic in fields such as industrial policy and technical education.

There is already an extensive network of North-South economic and policy co-operation links. The existence of two jurisdictions on the island is no more an insuperable barrier to freer trade between the two economies than any other difference in consumer preference, for example, varying standards of environmental regulation.

There will be serious problems for both Northern Ireland and the Republic of Ireland when, as now seems likely, a situation develops whereby the ROI is 'in' the euro but the UK remains 'out'. That said, it can still be argued that non-membership is the best option for the UK, and for Northern Ireland as part of the UK. The criteria set by the Labour Government in London to test whether the UK and Euroland economies have converged sufficiently to warrant UK entry to the euro are unlikely to be realised in the medium-term. Public opinion is still suspicious of the constitutional implications of the European project. In any event, Northern Ireland manufacturing output grew by a record 10 per cent in 1999-2000, demonstrating an ability to adapt to new markets.

In reality Northern Ireland firms do not face an 'either/or' decision when it comes to aiming for British as opposed to Republic of Ireland markets. They can and should follow the profit signals to the greatest commercial opportunities.

In short, the critical factor is the extent to which the Northern Ireland and Republic of Ireland economies are competitive in global markets. The great idea of an 'island economy' may be a nice marketing concept, but in substantive terms it can only make a comparatively minor contribution to increased economic competitiveness.

Acknowledgements

I am very grateful to the Northern Ireland Assembly Research and Library Service for some assistance in pulling out data. Any errors remain entirely my responsibility.

Notes

The Island Economy: Past, Present and Future: John Bradley

1 For an account of the reduction of tariff barriers affecting North-South trade that was carried out during 1956-62 prior to the Anglo-Irish Trade Agreement, see Kennedy, 1998.

2 At the time of writing — October 2000 — the weakness of the euro has driven the Irish pound to an all-time low against sterling.

3 Bardon, 1992 provides an account of the political, social and economic aspects of the rise of linen and ship-building in mid and late 19th century Belfast.

4 For a full treatment of the recent Southern growth experience, see Bradley *et al*, 1997 and Barry (ed.), 1990.

5 GDP at factor cost is a measure of the income of all the factors of production (labour as well as capital) that has been generated by domestic productive activities. It excludes taxes on expenditure such as excise duties and VAT, but includes subsidies. It also excludes financial flows from outside the domestic economy that occur (for example) through the current account of the balance of payments, such as profit repatriation by externally owned firms and inflows of financial aid such as the UK subvention to NI or EU Structural Fund aid.

6 The value of GDP in the Republic of Ireland can be distorted by the possibility of transfer pricing by foreign multinationals as they seek to locate as much profit as possible in Ireland through understating input prices. Of course, most of these profits subsequently flow out of the country.

7 In the year 1997, total GNP at current market prices was 13.1 per cent lower than GDP at current market prices in the Republic of Ireland.

8   It has been claimed by the Department of Economic Development that the cost of living in Northern Ireland is some 10 per cent below that of the UK as a whole, and that the UK and the Republic of Ireland have similar costs of living (*Irish Times*, December 10, 1998). However, since there are no reliable published regional price indices for the UK, it is difficult to evaluate this claim.

9   For data on the subvention, see Hutchinson, 1998. In the year 1995 the subvention was just over 24 per cent of GDP at factor cost (see below).

10   Of course, Northern Ireland has Objective 1 status and is also in receipt of investment aid from the EU as well as CAP subsidies. However, these are small compared to the level of the overall 'subvention'. The North received around £1 billion from the EU Structural Funds for the period 1994-99, i.e. around £200 million per annum over the five year period or 5 per cent of the annual subvention assuming complete additionality. The figures in the main text ignore these EU receipts.

11   Total net transfers from the EU to the Republic of Ireland amounted to about 4 per cent of GDP in 1995, and to 2.25 per cent if one excludes subsidy payments under the CAP. For details, see Bradley *et al*, 1997, p. 44.

12   The *Mezzogiorno* region of southern Italy has given its name to a phenomenon of underdevelopment and dependency that arose originally when the much richer northern Italian regions gave generous long-term income transfers to the south. This had an unintended side effect of locking the south into a low efficiency, low productivity, low entrepreneurial dependency (CEC, 1993).

13   Technically sales by Northern firms to Britain are not 'exports', but are classified as 'external sales'.

LYIT
LIBRARY
LETTERKENNY

The Island Economy: A Meaningful Concept? Esmond Birnie

1   For a careful evaluation of the European as compared to American models see *The Economist*, 16 September 2000.

2   In fact, economists in general do not have a distinguished record in predicting or recognising major developments. The post-war 1948–1973 so-called 'golden age' of full employment was not anticipated and, equally, there were few who foresaw the end of that era. Similarly, in the late 19th century W.S. Jevons thought Britain was about to run out of coal and in the mid 1970s there were plenty of predictions about the exhaustion of oil and other resources.

3   Hindley and Howe (1996) illustrate a method of assessing the financial impact of EU membership on the entire UK economy (i.e. allowing for inflows of Structural Funds, changes in investment flows and trade patterns, but also netting out the implied higher cost of food) which can then be adapted to the case of Northern Ireland as a region. Gudgin (1999) has estimated that at the upper limit EU membership represented a net addition to NI's resources equivalent to 3-4 per cent of regional GDP (this is something of an upper limit given the additionality problem - some of the incoming EU funds were undoubtedly 'matched' by a decrease in the UK Treasury monies which would otherwise have been available to the province). An equivalent figure for the Republic of Ireland would be around twice that in percentage terms.

4   Not all economists would necessarily accept this. According to endogenous growth theories, a well educated and trained work force can have continuous and dynamic effects (e.g. the productivity growth *rate* will be higher in addition to any once-off gain to the productivity *level*). Such assertions continue to cause controversy since they fly in the face of the assumption of diminishing returns which has been something of a mainstay of conventional economic theory for over a century. However,

at best, the case for the endogenous growth theories remains not proven.

5   There is a substantial literature in this area which has tended to attribute most European growth since 1945 to catch-up on the initially much higher American levels (see Denison for an early example and Crafts for a recent one).

6   In December 1999, with the transfer of executive power to a devolved administration in Northern Ireland, the Department of Economic Development (DED) was renamed the Department of Enterprise, Trade and Investment (DETI). Its remit, however, remained substantially as before.

7   The Industrial Development Board (IDB) has responsibility for inward investment promotion and medium and larger sized indigenous firms. The Local Enterprise and Development Unit (LEDU) is the small firms agency. The Industrial Research and Technology Unit (IRTU) grant-aids R and D and technology, and the Training and Employment Agency (TEA) is responsible for training and employment services.

8   There is evidence that few business executives in NI knew much about *Strategy 2010*'s existence and purpose several months after its publication.

9   Given the pervasive level of grant support for companies in Northern Ireland it is, in any case, open to dispute how *private* the NI private sector really is.

10 The agency is an umbrella body covering two organisations. IDA Ireland handles inward investment promotion while Enterprise Ireland has a broad remit for the indigenous sector (grant provision, technology policy, and overseas marketing and export support).

11 Notwithstanding the similarities between the documents, *Enterprise 2010* makes little mention of economic co-operation and policy co-ordination between Northern Ireland and the Republic. The NI document, *Strategy 2010,* includes more (though the amount is still small) on this subject. In

one sense this is ironic since the Republic's government has, at the *political* level, pushed the agenda of North-South links (hence Strand Two of the Good Friday Agreement). On the other hand, it is probably the case that *economically* North-South co-operation is more significant to the economy of Northern Ireland than to that of the Republic.

12   This is indicated by the intention to spend IR£40 billion within the 2000-2006 *National Development Plan*. Hitherto the spending allocations with the Republic's indicative national plans have tended to rely heavily on EU Structural Funds. In contrast, the 2000-2006 plan will be resourced mainly from national fiscal resources (the EU is to contribute IR£4.7 billion out of a total, including leveraged private spending, of IR£47 billion).

13   *Strategy 2010* describes itself as a draft plan which is to be presented to the Northern Ireland Assembly and Executive for amendment and/or approval. In the absence of a functioning Assembly and Executive throughout most of 1999-2000, that strategy was implemented piecemeal without the accountability and legitimacy which might otherwise have been afforded through a wider political discussion. There is, however, the potential for the Assembly (particularly the scrutiny committee for the relevant department) to conduct a thorough evaluation of *Strategy 2010*.

14   By 1958 there was co-operative management or administration of schemes such as the Foyle Fisheries Commission, the Erne hydro-electric scheme, cross-border electricity links and the Belfast-Dublin railway line.

15   The proposed all-Ireland political authorities were to be free-standing in the sense that they were not in any way to be accountable to a Northern Ireland Assembly and would derive their legislative authority and, presumably, funding arrangements from Dublin and London. Paragraph seven of the Strand Two proposals of the original Mitchell draft said: 'For the areas listed in annex C, where it is agreed that the new implementation bodies are to be established, the two governments are to make all

necessary legislative and other preparations to ensure the establishment of these bodies at the inception of the agreement ... such that these bodies function effectively as rapidly as possible' (Trimble 1998).

The unionist fear was that once such bodies came into being a united Ireland government would inevitably grow from this embryo.

'Annex C (of the Mitchell draft) listed eight bodies: Annexes A and B also listed respectively 25 and 16 other areas for immediate cross-border co-operation. Some of these were modest, but others included the harmonisation of further and higher education and general hospital services, as well as the creation of all-Ireland bodies to run trade and the arts' (Trimble, 1998).

16   The 10 April 1998 Agreement listed a dozen areas where co-operation through the North/South Ministerial Council might be possible: agriculture, education, transport, environment, inland waterways, social security/social welfare, tourism, EU programmes, inland fisheries, aquaculture and marine matters, health, urban and rural development.

17   My own experience during the talks about the North-South institutions during the September 1988-February 1999 period was that the SDLP felt compelled by pressure from Sinn Fein to include language. In the absence of such pressure, they might otherwise have pushed for a body on transport. The Republic's Government and the SDLP appeared to present a common front as to which bodies should be included (their draft position papers included the same list of proposed bodies in the same order!).

18   A similar point can be made by drawing a comparison with trade flows within the Iberian peninsula. In 1986 Spanish exports to Portugal were 2.2 per cent of its total and in 1997 still only 5.4 per cent. Portugal's population is about three times that of the Republic of Ireland and six times that of Northern Ireland.

19 As currently constituted, the North-South Ministerial Council seems to require universal agreement (as between the NI and Republic of Ireland delegations and *within* the NI delegation, where there is always cross-community representation) to any policy proposals.

20 In the long negotiations between the UUP and SDLP/ROI Government on the remit of the North-South Trade and Business Development Body during September 1998-February 1999, much hinged on this point.

21 This might prompt the question whether it was prudent for the Republic of Ireland to join the euro when the UK was not likely to be a member. There is some evidence that the Republic's macroeconomy is still more closely correlated to the UK trade cycle than say, the German trade cycle.

22 In the mid-1990s, the Ulster Unionist Party MP John Taylor opposed a possible Aer Rianta buy-out of the Belfast City Airport. Similarly there was some unionist unease in 2000 at proposals that the Tony O'Reilly-owned Independent Newspaper group was about to buy out the *Belfast Telegraph* (it was subsequently granted permission by the Department of Trade and Industry in London so to do).

Bibliographies

The Island Economy: Past, Present and Future: John Bradley

ABT *Northern Ireland: A Market Profile*, Dublin: An Bord Tráchtála. 1994.

Anderson, J. 'Integrating Europe, Integrating Ireland: The Socio-Economic Dynamics' in Anderson, J. and Goodman, J. (eds.) *Dis/Agreeing Ireland: Contexts, Obstacles, Hopes*, London: Pluto Press, 1998.

Association of European Border Regions *European Charter of Border and Cross-Border Regions*, Brussels: Association of European Border Regions, 1981.

Bardon, J. *A History of Ulster*, Belfast: The Blackstaff Press, 1992.

Barry, F. (ed.) *Understanding Ireland's Economic Growth*, London: Macmillan, 1999.

Barry, F. and Bradley, J. 'FDI and trade: the Irish host-country experience', *Economic Journal*, 107 (445), 1798–1811, 1997.

Bew, P. and Patterson, H. *Sean Lemass and the making of modern Ireland 1945–66*, Dublin: Gill and Macmillan, 1982.

Birnie, E. and Hitchens, D. 'An economic agenda for the Northern Ireland Assembly', *Regional Studies*, 32 (8), pp. 769–787, 1998.

Birrell, D. and Murie, A. *Policy and Government in Northern Ireland: Lessons of Devolution*, Dublin: Gill and Macmillan, 1980.

Blake, N. 'The Regional Implications of Macroeconomic Policy', *Oxford Review of Economic Policy*, 11, No. 2, 145–164, 1995.

Bradley, J. *An island economy: exploring long-term consequences of peace and reconciliation in the island of Ireland*, Dublin: Forum for Peace and Reconciliation, August, 1996.

Bradley, J. (ed.) *Regional economic and policy impacts of EMU: the case of Northern Ireland*, Research Monograph 6, April, Belfast: Northern Ireland Economic Council, 1998.

Bradley, J., FitzGerald, J., Honohan, P. and Kearney, I. 'Interpreting the Irish growth experience', in *Medium-Term review: 1997–2003*, Review no. 6, Dublin: The Economic and Social Research Institute, 1997.

Breen, R., Heath, A. and Whelan, C. 'Education and inequality in Ireland, North and South', in *Ireland, North and South: Perspectives from the Social Sciences*, Oxford: Oxford University Press, 1998.

Cadogan Group *Northern Limits: Boundaries of the Attainable in Northern Ireland Politics*, Belfast: The Cadogan Group, 1992.

Cecchini, P. *The European challenge 1992: the benefits of a Single Market*, London: Wildwood House, 1988.

Commission of the European Communities 'The economic and financial situation in Italy, Annex III: Regional disparities: the Southern issue', *European Economy*, Reports and Studies, No. 1, 1993.

D'Arcy, M. and Dickson, T. (eds.) *Border Crossings: Developing Ireland's Island Economy*, Dublin: Gill and Macmillan, 1995.

D'Arcy, M. *SME cross-border initiatives: their role in developing Ireland's island economy*, Study no. 2, *Border Crossings* project, December, 1998.

Fanning, R. *The Irish Department of Finance 1922–58*, Dublin: The Institute of Public Administration, 1978.

Farley, N. 'A Comparative Analysis of the Performance of the Manufacturing Sectors, North and South: 1960–1991', in *The Two Economies of Ireland:*

Public Policy, Growth and Employment, J. Bradley (ed.), Dublin: Oak Tree Press, 1995.

Government of Ireland *Economic Development*, Dublin: Stationery Office, 1958.

Hutchinson, G. 'Public expenditure in the regional economy of Northern Ireland: has the growth of the 1970s been sustained?', paper read to the Statistical and Social Inquiry Society of Ireland, October 22, 1998.

Kennedy, M. 'Towards co-operation; Sean Lemass and North-South economic relations: 1956–65', *Irish Economic and Social History*, XXIV, pp 42–61, 1998.

Molloy, S. (1995) 'Lever Brothers: The Reality of a Single Market', in *Border Crossings, Developing Ireland's Island Economy*, M. D'Arcy and T. Dickson (eds.), Dublin: Gill and Macmillan.

Monti, M. (1996) *The Single Market and Tomorrow's Europe*, London: Kogan Page, in association with the Commission of the European Communities.

Morishima, M. (1982). *Why Has Japan 'Succeeded'?*, Cambridge: Cambridge University Press.

Murphy, Anthony and Armstrong, David *A Picture of Catholic and Protestant Unemployed*, Belfast: CCRU, 1994.

NIEC (1992) *Inward Investment in Northern Ireland*, Belfast: Northern Ireland Economic Development Office.

Ohmae, K. (1996) *The end of the nation state*, London: Harper Collins.

O'Malley, E. (1998) 'The Revival of Irish Indigenous Industry 1987–1997', *Quarterly Economic Commentary*, April, Dublin: Economic and Social Research Institute.

Porter, M. (1990) *The Competitive Advantage of Nations*, London: Macmillan.

Quigley, G. (1992) *Ireland — An Island Economy*, paper presented at the Annual Conference of the Confederation of Irish Industry, Dublin, February 28, 1992.

Roche, P. and Birnie, E. (1995) *An Economics Lesson for Irish Nationalists and Republicans*, Belfast: Ulster Unionist Information Institute.

Smith, D. and Chambers, G. (1991) *Inequality in Northern Ireland*, Oxford: Clarendon Press.

Smyth, A. (1995) 'Transport: a hard road ahead', in *Border Crossings*, M. D'Arcy and T. Dickson (eds.), Dublin: Gill and Macmillan.

Trimble, D. (1998) Speech by First Minister to the *Chamber of Commerce of Ireland*, 19 November, Dublin.

Trimble, D. and Mallon, S. (1998) *Statement issued by the First Minister and Deputy First Minister towards implementing the Belfast Agreement*, as published in the *Irish Times*, Saturday, December 19.

The Island Economy: A Meaningful Concept? Esmond Birnie

Banking Ireland, 'Belfast-Dublin new economic axis', 23 September 1992.

Barry, F., *Understanding Ireland's Economic Growth*, Macmillan Press, 1999.

Belfast Telegraph, 'Northern Ireland's top 500', 18 February 1998.

Bew, P., H. Patterson and P. Teague, *Between War and Peace*, Lawrence and Wishart, 1997.

Birnie, J.E., 'The Economics of Unionism and Nationalism' in P.J. Roche and B. Barton (eds), *The Northern Ireland Question Nationalism, Unionism and Partition*, Ashgate, 1999, pp. 139–162.

Birnie, J.E. and D.M.W.N. Hitchens, *The Northern Ireland Economy*, Ashgate, 1999.

Birnie, J.E. and D.M.W.N. Hitchens, 'Nothing new under the sun: *Strategy 2010* in perspective', *Economic Outlook and Business Review,* vol. 15, no. 2, 2000, pp. 44–49.

Birnie, J.E. and D.M.W.N. Hitchens, 'Chasing the wind? Half a century of economic strategy documents in Northern Ireland' (forthcoming).

Bradley, J., 'Exploring long-term economic and social consequences of peace and reconciliation in the island of Ireland', *Forum for Peace and Reconciliation Consultancy Studies,* Stationery Office, 1996, no. 4.

Bradley, J., 'Evaluation of the ratio of unemployment rates as an indicator of fair employment: A critique', *Economic and Social Review,* vol. 28, no. 2, 1997, pp. 85–104.

Bradley, J., and D. Hamilton, 'Strategy 2010 Report by the Economic Development Strategy Review Group of Northern Ireland: A critical evaluation', *Paper,* Economic and Social Research Institute, 1999.

Business Eye, 'Editorial', September 1999, p.3.

Callan, T. and B. Nolan, 'Income inequality in Ireland in the 1980s and 1990s', in Barry, F. ed, *Understanding Ireland's Economic Growth,* Macmillan Press, 1999, 167–192.

CII , *Newsletter,* Confederation of Irish Industry, May, 1990.

Convery, F., 'Environment and energy', in Government of Ireland, *Ireland in Europe A shared challenge,* Stationery Office, Dublin, 1992, pp. 175–197.

Cooper and Lybrand/Indecon, '*A Corridor of Opportunity*', *Study of the Feasibility of developing a Belfast-Dublin Corridor,* Confederation of British Industry and Irish Business Employers Confederation, 1994.

Crafts, N.F.R, 'Some comparative aspects of Ireland's economic transformation', *Irish Banking Review,* Autumn, 1999, pp. 39–51.

Crowley, J., 'Transport', in Government of Ireland, *Ireland in Europe A Shared Challenge*, Stationery Office, 1992.

D'Arcy, M. and T. Dickson, *Border Crossings: Developing Ireland's Island Economy*, Gill and Macmillan, 1995.

DED, *Strategy 2010: A Draft Economic Policy Review*, Department of Economic Development, 1999.

Denison, E.F., *Why Do Growth Rates Differ?* Brookings Institute, 1967.

DTI 1999, *Our Competitive Future, UK Competitiveness Indicators 1999*, Department of Trade and Industry, Belfast.

Durkan, J., D. FitzGerald and C. Harmon, 'Education and growth in the Irish economy', in F. Barry ed, *Understanding Ireland's Economic Growth*, Macmillan Press, 1999, pp. 119–35.

Economist, The, 'Irish economy' 24 January 1987.

Economist, The, 'Spain and Portugal: Ever closer, inside Europe's Union', 14 February 1998.

Economist, The, 'Glittering economic prizes', 10 April 1999.

Economist, The, 'Europe's economies stumbling yet again', 16 September 2000.

Enterprise Ireland, *Strategy 1999–2001*, Department of Enterprise, Trade and Employment, 1998.

Fitzpatrick, J. and Mc Eniff, J., 'Tourism', in Government of Ireland, *Ireland in Europe A shared challenge,* Stationery Office, Dublin, 1992, pp. 119–152.

Forfás, *Enterprise 2010*, Forfás, Dublin, 2000.

Frameworks Document, The, 'Frameworks for the Future', Government of the UK and Government of Ireland, 1995.

Gillespie, A., 'Strategy 2010: Serious scrutiny recommended', *Economic Outlook and Business Review*, vol. 14, no. 2, 1999, pp. 35–42.

Gray, A.W.,'Industry and trade', in Government of Ireland, *Ireland in Europe A shared challenge*, Stationery Office, 1992, pp. 35–63.

Gudgin, G., 'EU membership and the Northern Ireland economy', in D. Kennedy ed., *Living with the European Union: The Northern Ireland Experience*, Macmillan Press, 1999, pp. 38–70.

Gudgin, G. and R. Breen, 'Evaluation of the ratio of unemployment rates as an indicator of fair employment', Central Community Relations Unit, 1996, *Research Report*, no. 4.

Hindley, B. and M. Howe, 'Better off out? The benefits and costs of EU membership', *Hobart Paper*, no. 99, Institute of Economic Affairs, 1996.

Hitchens, D., E. Birnie, A. McGowan, U. Triebswetter and A. Cottica, *The Firm, Competitiveness and Environmental Regulation: A Study of the European Food Processing Industry*, Edward Elgar, 1998.

Hitchens, D.M.W.N. and J.E. Birnie, *The Competitiveness of Industry in Ireland*, Avebury, 1994.

Hitchens, D.M.W.N. and J.E. Birnie, 'The potential for a Belfast-Dublin economic corridor', *Australasian Journal of Regional Studies*, vol. 2, no. 2, 1997, pp. 167–187.

Hitchens, D.M.W.N., K. Wagner and J.E. Birnie, *Closing the Productivity Gap: A Comparison of Northern Ireland, the Republic of Ireland, Britain and West Germany*, Gower-Avebury, 1990.

IEA, 'Regulating European labour markets: more costs than benefits', *Hobart Paper*, no. 138, Institute of Economic Affairs, 1999.

Irish Times, The, 'Europe's top banker delivers stern warning on inflation', 7 September 2000.

Irish Times, The, 'Unwise to dismiss Duisenberg warning', 12 September 2000.

Irish Times, The, 'Future of the EU lies in a union of independent sovereign states', 20 September 2000.

Kennedy, K.A., T. Giblin and D. McHugh, *The Economic Development of Ireland in the Twentieth Century*, Croom Helm, 1988.

Kennedy, M., 'Towards co-operation: Seán Lemass and North-South economic relations', *Irish Economic and Social History*, vol. XXIV, 1997, pp. 42–61.

Kennedy, P., *The Rise and Fall of the Great Powers: Economic Change and Military Conflict from 1500 to 2000*, Fontana, 1988.

Kinsella, R., 'Financial services', in Government of Ireland, *Ireland in Europe A shared challenge*, Stationery Office, Dublin, 1992, pp. 95–118.

Lal, D., 'The poverty of "development economics"', *Hobart Paperback*, no. 16, Institute of Economic Affairs, 1997.

MacEnroe, G. and W. Poole, 'Manufacturing: Two plus two makes more than four', in M. D.Arcy, and T. Dickson, ed., *Border Crossings*, Gill and Macmillan, 1995, pp. 110–2.

Mankiw, G., D. Romer and D. Weil, 'A contribution to the empirics of economic growth', *Quarterly Journal of Economics*, no. 107, pp. 407–38.

Matthews, A., 'Agriculture and natural resources', in Government of Ireland, *Ireland in Europe A Shared Challenge*, Stationery Office, Dublin, 1992, pp. 65–93.

McGurnaghan, M., and S. Scott, 'Trade and co-operation in electricity and gas', *Understanding and Co-operation in Ireland*, Paper IV, Co-operation North, Belfast and Dublin, 1981.

Michie, J., and M. Sheehan, 'The political economy of a divided Ireland', *Cambridge Journal of Economics*, vol. 22, 1998, pp. 243–59.

Munck, R., *The Irish Economy*, Pluto Press, 1993.

Murray, M. and J. Greer, 'The Republic of Ireland's National Development Plan 2000–2006: Some strategic planning implications for Northern Ireland', *Economic Outlook and Business Review*, vol. 15, no. 1, 2000, pp. 37–49.

NESC, 'Opportunities, challenges and capacities for choices', *Report*, no. 105, National Economic and Social Council, 1999.

NIEC, 'The implications of peripherality for Northern Ireland', *Report*, no. 111, Northern Ireland Economic Council, 1994.

NIEC, 'Regional economic and policy impacts of EMU: The case of Northern Ireland', *Research Monograph*, no. 6, Northern Ireland Economic Council, 1998a.

NIEC, 'The impact of a national minimum wage on the Northern Ireland economy: A response to the low pay commission', *Occasional Paper*, no. 9, Northern Ireland Economic Council, 1998b.

NIEC, 'Publicly funded R and D and economic development in Northern Ireland', *Report*, no. 133, Northern Ireland Economic Council, 1999a.

NIEC, 'A step-change in economic performance? A response to *Strategy 2010*', *Occasional Paper*, no. 12, Northern Ireland Economic Council, 1999b.

NIEC, 'Tough choices: Setting health and social care priorities in Northern Ireland', *Report*, no. 134, Northern Ireland Economic Council, 2000.

NIERC/DED/IDB, *Made in Northern Ireland. Sold to the World. Northern Ireland Sales and Exports 1994/95–1995/96*, Northern Ireland Economic Research Centre, Department of Economic Development, Industrial Development Board, 1997.

NIERC/DED/IDB *Made in Northern Ireland. Sold to the World. Northern Ireland Sales and Exports 1997/98–1998/99*, Northern Ireland Economic Research Centre, Department of Economic Development, Industrial Development Board, 1999.

Northern Ireland, *North/South Co-operation Implementation Bodies Northern Ireland Order 1999, Statutory Instruments*, The Stationery Office, London, 1999.

Ó Gráda, C., *Ireland: A New Economic History 1780–1939*, Oxford University Press, 1994.

Ó Gráda, C., and, K. O'Rourke, 'Irish economic growth, 1945–88', in N. Crafts and G. Toniolo (eds), *Economic Growth in Europe since 1945*, Cambridge University Press and Centre for Economic Policy Research, 1996, pp. 388–426.

Pollitt, M., 'The restructuring and privatisation of the electricity supply industry in Northern Ireland — will it be worth it?', *DAE Working Papers Amalgamated Series*, no. 9701 revised, 1997.

Porter, M., *The Competitive Advantage of Nations*, Free Press, 1989.

Rafferty, M., 'Northern Ireland and the Republic of Ireland: A contrast at firm level', in Gillespie, P. ed, *Britain's European Question: The Issues for Ireland: Seminar Papers*, Institute of European Affairs, 1996, pp. 83–85..

Roche, P.J. and J.E. Birnie, *An Economics Lesson for Irish Nationalists and Republicans* Ulster Unionist Information Office, 1995.

Scott, R., and M. O'Reilly, 'Exports of Northern Ireland manufacturing companies 1990', *NIERC Report*, Northern Ireland Economic Research Centre, 1992.

Simpson, J., 'Nearly a single market but not quite', *Business Belfast Telegraph*, 8 June 1993, p 4.

Trimble, D.,'Ulster should say "Yes"', *Daily Telegraph*, 13 April 1998.

Walsh, B., 'No room to be smug about productivity', *The Irish Times*, 15 September 2000.